THE SIX GATES OF COMPLETION

A Companion in Life's Transitions

by

BJ BROWN, MSW

Published by Integrity Arts Press
1637 28th Street, Boulder, Colorado 80301
www.IntegrityArtsPress.com

 Integrity Arts Press
Changing the World with Words

Integrity Arts Press publishes fiction and non-fiction rooted in the truth that living in integrity fuels joy, supports community, and promotes creativity. In addition to e-books and other electronic means of publishing, we are deeply committed to providing a kinesthetic option for our readers by publishing paper books that can be held, felt, written on, and maybe even hugged. Committed "green," we are ever mindful of our carbon footprint.

Cover Design by Brain Bolts
www.BrainBolts.com

Library of Congress Control Number: 2 0 1 1 9 2 5 9 1 3

ISBN: 978-0-9830506-3-6

FOR SHIRLEY

CONTENTS

The Six Gates of Completion

Acknowledgements

I sing praises for the world and for my ancestors.

To all those named and unnamed here, my heart is grateful for your inspiration, for being the breeze in my sails and sometimes my safe harbor. With love and gratitude, I thank my friends, family, clients, and colleagues for your support and faith in me and my life's work. I thank the Body Mantra community in Boulder, especially Kimberly Jonas, for every sacred dance and for your unconditionality. I deeply appreciate the rich and replenishing existence of Sound Circle—singing with you is my most profound healing elixir.

Thank you to the good people of Integrity Arts Press—Robbie Staufer, Kathy Kucsan, Kristie Steinbock—and especially my sweet friend and editor extraordinaire, Verna Wilder, and my genius graphics designer, Eric Boelts. I dearly appreciate you, Verna and Eric, for joining me on this most amazing and fun creative journey.

Big appreciation to Teri Charles, Jodi Patsiner, Robbie Staufer, and Kathy Kucsan for supporting me as readers, for cheering me on, and for your friendship. Thanks to friends Deb Batson and Babette DeLeonard for your keen proofing eyes. Thanks to photographer Nancy Stubbs for seeing me.

My appreciation to Gay Hendricks for the spark that started this creative project.

I acknowledge Mary Gay Shafer and Katie Hendricks, my dear teachers and friends, for always seeing me in my wholeness. I cherish your presence in my life.

I've been blessed with treasured friendships with Carol and Shirley. You opened your home and hearts to my presence, to witness Shirley from her last months to her last sacred breath on this earth. I'll forever remember Shirley asking me a few weeks before she died, "Tell me, what are the Six Gates? I want to hear all about it." I am exceedingly grateful to you both for allowing all of us so much loving space to complete with Shirley.

Sue Coffee - What am I gonna say? Thank you for knowing how to handle me, for reading this book from early on, and for your unwavering love and support.

My love and gratitude to my two children, Avery and Grayson. I learn from you every day, my big little teachers. My deepest gratitude to my beloved partner, Talia Spencer, *a mi me encanta, Natalia mia*. Thank you for loving me so well and for celebrating and encouraging my creative life. With all my heart and soul, I love you.

Foreword

What an outrageous adventure you're stepping into! You may think you've gotten a book about stuff and what to do about all of it lying around. This is not a book about getting things done. It is not a book about getting tidy, though you may find a certain serenity and spaciousness begin to co-habit with you as you read and breathe in these phrases. *The Six Gates of Completion* is about facing the abyss, going straight on through and finding sweet life reawakened on the other side. Many people have journeyed into the unknown and brought back treasures that you can find in museums, the artifacts of what cultures valued and how they expressed the mysteries. When you take this journey with BJ as guide, you'll enter your own treasure house and uncover amazement under the dust. Most people don't complete because they're afraid there's nothing else under the tangles of incompletion, that their lives are ordinary and dull, that magic exists only in the movies. BJ will be fully with you through each gate to magic by looking through the ordinary into the possibilities of daily divinity.

You are about to savor more than head or heart wisdom. You are about to enter a cozy kitchen (the best place for all kinds of nurturing) where soul wisdom will tingle your nerve endings and change the way you view your life. BJ has traveled fully in the outer and inner realms, and just like in the best travel books, can evoke a full sensory experience through her words.

I learned many years ago not to personally meet authors whose work I admired, as they so often practiced the "do what I say, not what I do" school of writing. In recent years society has experienced many dramas of unrevealed lives, of secrets maintained behind a false front, and it has cost all of us. BJ radiates this new paradigm of transparency and unity. It is time now to celebrate wholeness, to model and practice the art of alignment. With BJ, in person and through this book, you benefit from her living integrity. She has experienced what she asks you to explore. She has jumped, fallen, swooned, and gathered where she asks you to do something unimaginable. You can find your own entirety as you journey with BJ through the gates she has opened.

Of the many life experiences that illuminate this book, the ones that will possibly surprise you come from capturing the extraordinary in the daily pulsations that each of us encounters. BJ is a master of turning experience into creative expression, and she'll guide you to become your own master. I've seen her amazing collages, the way she turned an office into a sanctuary, and the many times her presence has opened the gates of healing for her clients and friends. Feeling the same quality of wonder and discovery evoked from these pages expands my breath into a satisfied "ahhh." I am confident that wonder awaits you as you dive in and ride to your own wizardry.

Kathlyn Hendricks, Ph.D., BC-DMT
Director of Training, The Hendricks Institute
Co-Author of *Conscious Loving*,
The Conscious Heart, and *Attracting Genuine Love*

Prologue

This book has been in the making since 1994, though I didn't know that fully until one morning late in September of 2007. I woke with the words surging through me, landing on the page almost too quickly for my hand to carry them. I recognized in those first hours and days of writing that pieces of discussion, musings, and dreams I'd had over time about being a writer, and on what subject, were now coming to fruition.

Over the course of about the last twenty years I've had many occasions to visit with channelers, astrologers, shamans, psychics, energy workers, and other healing practitioners with a leaning toward the esoteric or Eastern healing modalities. Many told me that they saw me in service to others, that I had a great deal to offer, and that I was meant to expand my scope and sense of responsibility to serve. I listened with what I called a healthy skepticism. Now I refer to it as discernment. Some of these practitioners said that I was to write a book and allow my offering to reach more people than those I saw only in my private practice.

One astrologer in particular encouraged me to publish a book. "Where's the book?" she'd bark, "It's right here in your chart!" As I look back on it now, I recall feeling a "yikes" inside me. I wasn't ready. At that time in my life I was run by fear about being a writer. Between 1995 and 1998 I'd composed six songs. I arranged and published two of them for women's a cappella ensembles. While I appreciate my own efforts and the results of this accomplishment, arranging music was a grueling experience for me. Part of my choosing a difficult process was that these songs came through, full out, all parts and rhythms— there they were, singing in my head and in my heart. While I totally delighted in the music coming through me in this way, I didn't have either the computer software or skills to plunk it out and have these notes conveniently drip out of my printer. I chose the old-fashioned way and sat at a piano, tapping out a few notes at a time and then noting them with pencil in their rightful place on staff paper.

I am a singer. I was barely getting myself around the idea of being a composer, much less the notion of being an author, though I'd written nearly every day since I was in my late teens. After several months, I went back to the astrologer, who asked me again where the book was. "Couldn't it be the songs?" I pleaded. The astrologer looked down at the astrological charts and updates. She pondered with a "hmmm," made a "sthtsst" sound with her tongue on her teeth. Then she bellowed, poking the pencil down on the chart, "Nope, Honey. It says right here that you're supposed to write a book. You've got to reach more people, Darlin'!" In deep appreciation for her wisdom, encouragement, and enthusiasm, I thanked her. She died several years ago. I imagine her boisterously and gleefully saying in spirit, "I told you!"

Allow me to welcome you through this portal. I have experienced closure, deaths of many loved ones, health issues, endings, and completions, all too numerous to mention. A few of these events could be their own books. I have passed through transitions, sometimes with great resistance or suffering, sometimes in utter denial that anything was ending or changing at all. Some of these transitions have felt excruciatingly beautiful. I have also been the gatekeeper, if you will, for many others' passages, whether as guide, witness, or teacher in their life transformations or by aiding and witnessing their dying. Each experience has been of great value to me, each a blessing. There are also the rare events on my journey that were truly pivotal in my consciousness and soul growth, the kind that launch and alter a life in such a transformative spin that it seems words could never truly describe. My hope is for this book to convey the profundity of that which is ineffable. Perhaps it will allow you to see the ordinary to be extraordinary. Perhaps the extraordinary may begin to color the ordinary.

Each completion has refined my capacity to be here now and offer myself as the gatekeeper for you as you face your completions consciously. I've not always moved through my own transitions or met the end of certain times with as much grace or awareness as I intend for myself now. In some cases I did poorly, to be sure. These more awkward experiences are just as refining, as much a gift, a chance for discovery. Sometimes we don't sustain the level of integrity we aspire to, which can teach us humility. These times may be of more service to us than those we judge as positive experiences if we allow ourselves to come to that situation again with a commitment to meet it with an open mind, open heart, and sense of responsibility, which is not to say fault or blame. We'll explore "responsibility" together later in this book.

How freeing it will be when you empower yourself to meet your own truth with a sense of self-responsibility! If this feels like something you truly want for your life and you are experiencing deep fear, or you are aware of trauma that is still easily stirred, please seek support to accompany you along the way. I recommend someone who is open to holistic views, spiritual mentoring, or body-centered coaching or psychotherapy. I've noted some resources in the back of this book. You may also choose to do this exploration with a learning buddy or a small group of companions, fellow explorers who are on a similar conscious path. This journey can be enhanced when you invite someone to be a witness, someone with whom you may be a deep listener.

As you read this book, let the layers unfold at your own pace. Pushing is one way to remain unfinished, attached, which we will address later. If you approach the page (the one you read or the one on which you write your Self) with an inner sense of patience, curiosity, and openness to discovery, you are more apt to create ease in your process.

You'll be invited to do some excavating as you traverse The Six Gates. You might want to bring along a hard hat, some gloves, and a flash light. Some extra tissues may also come in handy.

Welcome yourself to it now. I appreciate you and invite you to appreciate your own courage and commitment to step even more surely on a path of love and integrity.

May you go gently, patiently, fiercely, and with compassion for yourself and others.

૭   ૭   ૭

୨ ୨ ୨

INTRODUCTION

୨ ୨ ୨

৭   ৭   ৭

We often cross the most profound thresholds in life with no road maps. We embark on life's most cherished or most difficult transitions without handy guidebooks or tools for creating change with greater ease. *The Six Gates of Completion* provides a clear path for a grounded sense of living in completeness, for facing transitions while expanding into the life we most want to create.

Part I answers questions about what completion is and is not. We'll also look at how to become more internally resourced and enhance sensory awareness. Completion is a state of being that carries its own experience felt in your heart, mind, and body. Part I reveals ways of tuning in to the wisdom of your body. Attaining this state of sensory acuity can create a felt satisfaction for completing anything from a creative project to saying goodbye to a loved one in their dying. We may feel complete at the end of a relationship that allowed both partners to say honestly and truly all that needed to be said, free of regret or malice. In Part I, we'll also visit four kinds of primary incompletions.

In Part II, I highlight teachings on how to reach healthy states of completion through what I call the "Six Gates of Completion." Throughout the book you'll find vignettes, instructions, and exercises that pave a path for increased ease through transitions, great and small.

You wake in the morning and yield to rest at night. In flows a breath, and then you release it, mostly without conscious awareness. A son's passage from second grade to third or a girl's rite of passage as her body shifts to womanhood—these are significant life transitions for them as well as for the parents witnessing them. Approaching a difficult meeting or test, coming home from retreat or vacation, entering deep commitment with a partner, completing a project, moving from and into a new home or career, a divorce, a death, a birth—all are profound transitions. They are ordinary, and they are extraordinary. Any twist or turn of the day, movement from here to there in everyday chores, are junctures, transitions that we might do with ease, or strenuously, depending on what's happening internally at that moment. These countless shifts in our day or in our lifetime have simultaneous stops and starts and in-between places. You are invited to wonder on the places, events, and relationships in your life that feel incomplete, left unfinished. The journey is constant. The paradox is that there really are no beginnings and no endings. Change innately means an end of something and a beginning of something else. If there is anything you can count on it is the constant nature of change itself.

In Part III you'll be given an opportunity to look more deeply into your Self with the guiding encouragement of what I call Soul Play. The Soul Play exercises may challenge or tease the deeper places within your being and your body, within your sensations and your heart, to bring what is your unarguable truth to the foreground. I encourage you to keep a journal to free your ongoing self-inquiry. Journaling creates a sacred space in which to convey your inner landscape, a place where deep expression may be held in a container that is private and for your own reflection. Your journal can be a creative sanctuary. If you prefer, you can do the exercises in the space provided for your spontaneous process right there in Part III.

You may often be called to come back to the book and the Soul Play exercises. What you visit today as you explore the questions may likely be a stepping stone, only partial truths emerging. The responses you give tomorrow, next month, next year may have shifted. You might find they've become deeper and vaster. They may later hold even sweeter vulnerability, truth, and a greater sense of completion.

The Six Gates of Completion is a guide to accompany your whole Self as you traverse a path of integrity. Let it be like a gentle whisper of a friend, or the roar of the ocean, coming to you and through you with waves of possibility, peace, love, and appreciation.

As you move through the Six Gates, you'll notice that I include events from my own life as examples, perhaps models, for how to and how not to move through the transforming turns in life, big or small. Certain things had to unfold in my life, even pierce my heart, before I could write this book. I've had a number of different types of relationships shift and change, and a few that broke apart. The greatest loss in my youth was the sudden death of my mother when she was quite young, and so was I. I held the hand of my friend as he was released from life support. He was among several I knew who died of AIDS in the '80s. Many other dear friends, relatives, and pets have died along the way. The most profound transitions of my life thus far are these: My mother's death; my recovery from drug and alcohol addiction; creating my family with my Beloved partner and my two stepchildren; the reconciliation with my father and later his death. These experiences have served and blessed me beyond measure and in turn have served many others. May you find them useful as well.

෨   ෨   ෨

PART I:

WHAT IS COMPLETION?

෨   ෨   ෨

❧   ❧   ❧

Completion is a natural and organic portal through which we pass again and again. How do we benefit by living in completion? In doing so we create more grace, integrity, and awareness as we come to the beginnings, transitions, and endings we all must naturally face.

Completion is the state of knowing that at the end of the day, we've left nothing unsaid. We feel free of regret, resentment, remorse. We feel confident we have followed our heart and our integrity. We have no loose ends. We have clearly expressed our love and the significant people in our life have heard or felt our love.

We can step into a state of completion throughout ordinary and extraordinary times. The more we become practiced at moving through the most mundane of transitions with ease and a sense of completion, the more refined and skilled we'll become at times that are most profound and life altering.

11

In all of nature and within the human condition is the innate urge toward completion. Some of us are resistant to the inevitable and consistent tides of change; even so, change has its way with us, moving us to complete and begin, repeatedly. Ultimately, to feel complete means to feel fulfilled. That sense of completion creates the opening for the next thing to flow toward us. The next project, the next conversation, the next recycling week, a new home, another creative endeavor, a new love, the greetings and goodbyes—whatever they are, we can meet all such transitions with greater satisfaction when we honor the natural urge toward completion. We can come to the end of our day, the end of our lives, and know fulfillment. These pages are meant to unlock your inner knowing and sensation about what completion and fulfillment feel like to you personally, in your own heart, mind, and body.

When I think of how it is to feel complete, all sorts of examples pop up, such as cleaning out my desk, paying bills, finishing a creative project, putting away the clean laundry, kissing my kids goodnight. These are very ordinary and even mundane things we do. They are satisfying nonetheless. We can learn to cultivate a sense of satisfaction while taking care of ordinary tasks or taking on important endeavors. The key element is to bring our attention, conscious awareness, into the project at hand. The Soul Play exercises in Part III offer you opportunities to enhance your awareness about the process of completion.

Extraordinary transitions also come to mind, those endings or beginnings that shape our lives beyond what we could possibly have imagined. These are the births and deaths, the miraculous and tragic events we experience. Living "complete" makes us open to welcoming the new paths that cut through our story, as well as giving us an inner fortitude for thriving through the devastating losses. Again, our intention and increased awareness on these transitional times will enhance the quality and value these experiences have on us.

Living in a state of conscious completion requires that we commit to be tuned in with ourselves to discern when we feel complete and when we do not feel complete. This hearty intention to be more aware of completion and incompletion is the key to unlocking those blocked and contracted places where we are feeling stuck, undone—incomplete. For example, it is a good beginning step to notice at the end of the day if you are feeling uncomfortable inside yourself, a glitch in your body. Do you have a nagging feeling that something feels undone, unfinished? A commitment to completion calls us to face into those unfinished pieces in our lives, instructing us about what needs our attention or what needs to be expressed.

Setting Intentions

One way to increase your awareness throughout your day is to set an intention when you wake up. Pause in the beginning of your day to tune in. Ask yourself what you want for the day. Set a clear intention for how you want to be in your interactions. Here are a few examples: "It's my intention for the day to pay attention to my body." Or "I intend to listen to my sensations as I move through my day." Or "I intend to appreciate something about those with whom I interact today, even if I get annoyed with someone." "My intention today is to listen for when I'm truly feeling a Yes or a No from the inside out." Once you agree with yourself, feeling clear about what you want to create and the sorts of intentions you want to make, your capacity and strength to be in a state of integrity is expanded. You are on to yourself. It's a fine course in deepening a sense of a healthy conscience and consciousness.

What does your list look like? Were there any specific transitions in your day to which you can give more attention than you did in that moment? Your wondering on that specific transition now is one proactive step to get complete about it within yourself.

When we honor the transitions in our life with deeper attention, we attain a sense of fulfillment. Through the births and deaths, from how we run a business to how we raise our children, and woven through our relationships, we can achieve fulfillment. What if we simply choose to befriend the ordinary and extraordinary inevitable changes in our lives, wide-awake and sensitively alert to what we most value? Even when we do not "get" what we think we want, this wakeful attention and intention to create completion is one road to fulfillment.

Changes Great and Small

Completion brings on and is a result of transitions. Let's look at the myriad ways in which transitions—and so completion—could show up:

- ๑ Waking up in the morning
- ๑ Saying goodbye to loved ones for the day
- ๑ Heading to work or school
- ๑ Moving from class to class, meeting to meeting
- ๑ Returning home
- ๑ The shifts from the end of the work day to bedtime
- ๑ The turn of the season
- ๑ Our children moving from one grade to the next
- ๑ Getting kids or elders to and from various appointments or activities
- ๑ Coming into and through the holidays
- ๑ Graduating from high school or college
- ๑ Entering into a retreat or vacation and returning home again
- ๑ Beginning or completing a project; completing the many stages within the project
- ๑ Beginning or ending with a mentor, therapist, or coach

There are countless transitions that weave through a day or a lifetime. Then there are the life-transforming, or perhaps earth-shaking, transitions:

- ❧ Birth of a child
- ❧ Our children's growth spurts
- ❧ Changes in our bodies
- ❧ Sexual identity and sexual orientation
- ❧ Moving to a new home
- ❧ Divorce
- ❧ Change of career
- ❧ Abortion or miscarriage
- ❧ Marriage
- ❧ New wealth or financial crisis
- ❧ Loss or death of a pet
- ❧ Illness
- ❧ Global climate change
- ❧ Aging (a loved one or our own)
- ❧ The process of dying and death (a loved one or our own)

There is no way to describe the vastness of every shift in a day, let alone in a lifetime. When we begin to wonder how we are moving through the thresholds of a day, we may get a glimpse into how we face those events that have a greater effect on the whole of our life.

Intend to live your life in a state of completion and you will come to see transition and closure as something to be treasured. Completing even the simplest tasks grants us satisfaction and fulfillment. Completion is like a surprise, like those turns in music when the rhythm shifts. These changes in a piece of music—including the rests, the silence, the pause between movements—are what make it whole, just as completion honors the small and great transitions in life. This is how we live life to the fullest.

Be Here and Now

As we contemplate the patterns or styles of making transitions, the endings, the shifts in a day or in a life, we are likely to have some epiphanies rise from personal history. Events from childhood will resurface in our memory. We may experience physical or emotional responses to these recollections. For example, as we delve into the desire to understand healthy transition, we may recall a transition from childhood that lacked awareness or a sense of closure. Residual feelings of grief, anger, the ache in the gut, fears, or nervousness can come into our experience as though the event were happening again now. Let these feelings come up and flow through your awareness. Hold an intention to have them provide information about your process. The emotional and physical urgings are opportunities for you to come to a sense of completion, to move through those events in your past. Let the waves of emotion teach you rather than keep you from moving on.

As another example, some of you may have learned not to trust yourself in part because you observed your mother not trusting herself. Perhaps you witnessed her acquiesce when you sensed she wanted something else. Some may discover they had a father who shut down his feelings, overriding his needs, overworking, perhaps, or simply too armored to show his vulnerability. Now you see yourself similarly overriding what you want or withholding your own emotional expression. Most families run on certain spoken and unspoken rules. Some families are bound by secrets, shrouded by acts of abuse, rage, or the threat of harm to one's true and essential nature. These discoveries are not to direct blame for how it is now, nor even for how it was then. The discoveries can, however, explain how one might take on certain patterns of expression and behavior. These patterns and even beliefs are imprinted and inherited, generation to generation. Our conscious choice and responsibility are not present when we are tiny ones, and in fact, these patterns may already be set into the fabric of our being when we are toddlers. There is good news, however: there is a surging, compelling force that moves the heart and soul. The soul wants to outdo the ego, thrive above and beyond the drama and complaint. Essence, allied with soul, naturally wants to shine through any hurt or darkness from our past.

Now, this moment, is all you have. Drs. Gay and Kathlyn Hendricks of the Hendricks Institute in California teach the following exercise in their Foundations Training (for more information, go to www.hendricks.com): As you permit memories and feelings to flow through you, say to yourself, allowing yourself to hear your own voice, "That was then and this is now." As you say, "That was then," point away from yourself. As you say, "This is now," bring your hand back to yourself, placing your hand on your body or over your heart. Moving, gesturing, and placing your hand on your body helps to anchor the true and positive statement: This is now.

What follows is a brilliant example offered by one of the apprentice graduates of the Hendricks Institute for Conscious Living. She describes how she moved through painful memories using the process of "that was then" to ground herself in the present. She writes:

When I was six years old I was sexually abused by my cousin who was about 10 years older than me. I've done a lot of personal growth work about this over the last 20 years, and today I received an amazing gift.

My cousin died 18 years ago. I had brought a rose to put on his grave and stood there for a while feeling sad and angry. Then I felt a wave of anger and tears and I wanted to kick the gravestone, so I snarled and growled at it and swore at it. It felt good. Then I pointed at the grave with my right hand and said, "That was then." I took a few steps, turned around, and with my left hand pointed at myself and said. "This is now." I felt relieved. I did this sequence a few more times and felt grief, sadness, more anger, and then stillness. With every round I felt lighter. When I felt complete, I laid the rose on his grave and again I said, "That was then" and as I turned I said, "This is now." I had a sense of my six-year-old self standing to my right and looking up at me smiling. My six-year-old took my hand and together we walked away. I didn't expect to be reunited with the six-year-old part of me, and I felt a flood of warm feelings of joy, deep gratitude, and excitement rush up my spine. It was an unexpected gift to find her there and to walk away with her by my side.

I feel full, and a sense of wholeness fills my entire being.
I feel grateful for this work and for being on this journey.
~ D.

༄ ༄ ༄

Closure—completion. I have experienced and witnessed countless profound shifts like D.'s. Hers is an example of how commitment, desire, and action allowed someone to peel away layers of wounds to reveal her authentic nature. I appreciate her deeply for being a legacy breaker and for permitting us to witness her courageous journey.

In our adult lives, barring physical or mental debilitation, we have conscious choice and we have a responsibility to listen to ourselves and claim our own path. Parents and families are teachers, whether they appear to us as such or not. We can learn how to do things beautifully, how to attend to our own lives, our bodies, our homes, and our own children by how sensitively and consciously our parents raised us. Or we learn by the perfection of their imperfections. Their wounded or unconscious ways of raising us become the teaching for how to live from kindness and integrity.

I've often found in my work that most people have developed certain patterns that were not innately their own. It's as though we have an inner knowing, an essential truth within us that says such things as "I don't understand why I behave this way" or "I'm confused and feeling foggy about how I'm reacting right now." Another common pattern is that many of us have learned to say yes when the real answer is no. Our bodies attempt to sequence positive and negative patterns through our whole being, mostly without our conscious awareness. Whether we're carrying a pattern that is energetically healthy or toxic, our system naturally wants to move it through, much like our body knows how to let a cold run its course. Negative patterns can cause delay, avoidance, or resistance to creating healthy transition and completion.

On an unconscious level, our physical, spiritual, mental, and emotional systems are moving through everything we experience to correct or heal something we learned and took on from our primary caregivers. This inner knowing goes on to coax us toward something more true, more authentically ourselves. Here is where the commitment is crucial. A survival mechanism can kick in for many people at this point. It can be terrifying to break the undesired, unhealthy pattern. For some people, there can be a contraction, hardening and holding onto the very pattern from which they long to recover. It is possible that a trusted professional, teacher, or spiritual counsel is necessary to assist us through to that healing and recovery. Only we can choose and commit and choose again and recommit. Commitment and intention toward a happier, thriving, more loving experience of life can be like a magnet, pulling us back on course.

Only you can tell if you are creating ease on your journey. I'm not saying, necessarily, that we will utterly cease to have stress or cease to feel grief when particular events arise. That is not the aim. I am saying let's create smoother transitions, be more present, tender, and compassionate with ourselves and others. As inner strength grows, we drop the ego-based ways of armoring our vulnerable parts. Self-confidence and trust create a truer sense of what is our Yes and what is our No. As you tune in more and commit to your own true nature, you'll pass through and integrate the little shifts as well as the big, hairpin turns of your life. Increased awareness for and through transitions makes for healthy, more fulfilling experiences of completion.

False Completion

It's important to look at the ways we mask an interaction or gesture as completion. Here's an example: You think you are done with someone. You mask the falsehood of that, maybe even calling it closure or completion. You dodge him at the office, you don't return her calls, or you ignore them, saying to yourself, "I'll have nothing to do with that person." This is a masquerade for completion. It may be that we've not yet learned the intricacies of what it is to come to completion or to feel resolved. But this false completion is still a cover for unresolved feelings.

A masquerade for resolution would include thoughts like this: "Well, I got my way that time." "Boy, he got his." "Ha—I showed them." "I'm done!" "I have nothing more to say and too bad about him." Digging your heels into a mound of righteous indignation does not bring you full circle to resolution or closure. This is a false sense of power as well as a false sense of completion.

Take a look into your own laboratory of experience. Think of a situation where you just knew you were right, and every time this person or event comes up in your mind your blood boils, your energy escalates, and you dance around trying to convince anyone who will tolerate you speaking at them that you have been wronged. Can you feel the energy of tangling yourself up with such beliefs? This may be creating a charge, an adrenaline rush, a false sense of getting attention, an attachment to being stressed and unhappy. In an attempt to step into your personal power, you have created a false sense of power and control. This is not creating completion, nor is it doing anything for your health, your soul, your growth, or your joy. In fact, this way of staying hooked into such a pattern may be an unconscious attempt at staying falsely connected to the person involved or to that time in your life. It may even be an unconscious, shadowy route to create healing. Why not experiment in a direction that has more ease?

We've all heard of, or maybe been through, the "bad divorce," where we struggle and repeat unresolved stories and drama. I see this as the frayed thread that keeps people hooked into each other energetically and psychically; it is the unconscious attempt to stay connected. When we cling to the negative communications and are attached to getting our way, we are creating entanglement, not happiness or connection.

Some people may be in a dynamic that is unsafe, where one is abusive or addicted to something that makes it impossible for them to communicate or listen.

Sometimes the person with whom we want or need completion has died. We still have opportunities to clear anything that remains within us that is toxic or unfinished. When our heart and mind are open to the quality of commitment and intention I've described, we can make a clear path to move on from what has been stored up inside us. Sometimes we can't engage in direct communication with the other party. We may find that in some situations we can't match our commitment or we take responsibility for their part. We cannot do closure for another. This is about freeing ourselves up for a healthier life, which of course can have a positive impact on others.

When I was 15 years old, my mother died suddenly of a heart attack when she was 42. She had smoked since she was a teenager, and I was already a smoker by the time she died. I continued to smoke for another 13 years or so. I also became severely addicted to alcohol and drugs. My mother drank. Smoking and drinking was highly accepted, even expected in some social circles from about the late 50's to 70's. I suspect she may have been an alcoholic.

The early stages of my recovery revealed my own longing to keep my mother close somehow. Clinging to these unhealthy—even life threatening—behaviors gave me the illusion that I could be connected with her. I believe I was making an unconscious attempt to save her or bring her back, either by ultimately saving my own life or by joining her through my slow suicide of drug addiction and alcoholism. As you can see, I chose the former. I did so, however, with the recognition that mine was the only life I could save.

Truly grieving and loving my mother, facing my loss of her without being in a substance-induced altered state, was absolutely vital. Completion from the long held angst of a life-altering event was vital, as well as a primary teaching for me to then use in my own service and work in the world. I had to accept that this self-destructive path was no way to keep her close. Clean and sober since 1986, I stepped fully into my health and recovery, thriving in my own body and life. More now than ever I can feel her in my heart, and I have closure.

Incompletion

To be at loose ends is to feel incomplete, unfinished. The body provides signals through feelings and sensations to confirm the sense of unfinished for us. We sometimes think, "I'm at loose ends" or "I feel like I'm forgetting something." Is there a project we haven't yet completed? Perhaps we feel uncertainty about how to move forward. We might have unfinished business in any number of areas in life, such as in relationships, with family or friends, or at work. Feeling incomplete can be about something as mundane as not having cleared the desk or not returning phone calls. Maybe you have yet to create the life you want or to express yourself as fully as you desire, which would also evoke a sense of being at loose ends—incomplete.

In his audio presentation called "The Manifestation Course—Advanced Techniques for Creating Abundance in Love and Money," Gay Hendricks discusses the "law of completion" and the four primary areas of incompletion.

- ❧ Promises not kept.
- ❧ Actions you feel guilty about.
- ❧ Important unspoken communications.
- ❧ Significant resentments or regrets.

Each of these areas of incompletion leaves loose ends that deplete our energy and hinder the natural flow of manifestation in our lives.

Unkept Promises

A promise is similar in vibration and energy to a vow or a commitment. When we make a promise to someone, there is not only the practical and physical expression of giving our word to follow through on something. There is also the energetic cord that connects us to that agreement and the person to whom we gave the promise.

Breaking an agreement or betraying a commitment creates an energetic drain that is like a dangling cord of energy. An unkept promise is something we have left at loose ends, an agreement we made but have not honored. When we make an agreement with someone, we also make it with ourselves. When an agreement or promise is broken, it causes a leak of energy between the parties involved and within the person who made the agreement to begin with. Whether the promise was made yesterday or decades ago, if it is still left hanging—that is, if no words have been spoken or no responsibility taken to address the agreement—there is a gap yet to be closed.

Still Holding Guilt

How do we know when we are feeling guilty? This is something to consciously check in about, tune into the body's sensations. It's been my experience that when someone feels guilt, it is because they still feel bad for some action they took that caused hurt to another or because they feel they deceived or betrayed someone. Another explanation for guilt is that it accompanies an experience of being shamed. People feel bad because they often carry the severe judgments of others.

Explore something else instead—the felt sense of remorse. Remorse is a quality of feeling that is more from the heart, a feeling of sadness for an action that had a negative effect on another. Guilt is not a feeling —it is a perception we get stuck in. It is a state based in fear and dependent on our perceptions of what we have done to another or feelings we have been shamed into experiencing. In that sense, it is an "other-referenced" state. Remorse comes from feeling genuine sorrow and comes from within—that is, remorse is self-referenced.

Important Unspoken Truths

What communication are you withholding? Is there something you have left unsaid? Again, it could be a recent or distant past event that stirred some action, experience, or feeling that was stuffed down into a pocket that remains tucked away in the mind, heart,

and body. Our physical system, the body, certain
relationship dynamics, inform us that something is
caught inside and must be expressed, a truth revealed.

The mind can trick us into all sorts of excuses
about why it's better to withhold the untold
communication—but there is a difference between
secrecy and privacy, and our bodies know it. Some
examples I hear are, "Well, I just wanted to protect
him" or "I know she couldn't understand" or "I knew it
would make them so angry and I thought I'd be
punished" or "There's no way she could handle it." The
list goes on.

The energy it takes to hold on to a secret causes
the whole body to contract. This makes us not fully
available for life and intimate relationships. We may
think something is going on "out there" that causes
our suffering or disappointment. If you are holding
onto something, it is likely to place a wedge firmly
between self and loved ones, not to mention between
self and one's own presence and joy.

Significant Regrets and Resentments

These four primary incompletions can show up in various ways—on their own, all four together, or in pairs. When you imagine what you are feeling regret about, notice the quality of emotion and sensation.

Answer these questions before continuing.

What do you become aware of when you think about your regret?

_____

_____

_____

_____

_____

_____

_____

_____

How do you notice regret in your body?

_____

_____

_____

_____

_____

_____

_____

_____

_____

The thing you regret stirs a sensation of longing to cleanse the situation. This can be done through the formula of Six Gates of Completion. It's here, though, that a genuine apology would serve you and the other party well. What goes deeper is an overt indication that you understand what may have caused some hurt or broken promise. This conscious awareness gives an apology more substance. It shows the other that your behavior has shifted and that you are making an authentic commitment from integrity and consciousness. What goes a greater distance than the apology in healing and completion, and is received as more meaningful, is an expression of feeling, such as the remorse we spoke of earlier. For example, if I come to recognize that something I said was harsh toward someone, I'm listening for the feeling in myself about my behavior and then expressing that to the person. It might sound something like, "I feel sad that I spoke to you that way and I see it was hurtful to you" or "I feel sad about my behavior and I'm scared you're still angry with me." Owning your behavior in this way elicits a true apology rather than the glib, "Sorry about that."

Resentments are about holding onto anger about something or toward someone. Resentment is different from anger; resentment carries the feeling of "done wrong," for instance. Resentment often arises when we make an agreement we didn't want to make. Resentment is fueled by a single act or through ongoing behaviors that we do not want to be doing. A classic example is when we say yes when the answer is really no.

When someone asks something of us and we say yes when the answer is truly no, we are bound to feel resentment. Resentment also comes up disguised as being about the other person. We may feel anger for being asked for too much, being overly tasked by others. If you say to yourself or out loud, "I can do it," when you already know you are busy or tired or have to rush to some other appointment, then you are likely saying yes when the real answer is no. This may sound like selfishness; however, if you have any inclination to respond to these words with thoughts of obligation or a fear that things would fall apart if you took better care of yourself, then you are a likely candidate for carrying resentment. Try on a new way. Explore the possibility that being centered in Self (not self-centered) is a great gift to yourself as well as to others. If you are driven by obligation, you run a high risk of lacking the ability to be fully present for your own good life, as well as diminishing your capacity to be truly present and engaged in healthy, loving relationships.

True Signs

We have the greatest faculty always available to guide us through change and toward that felt sense of completion. Our human system of feeling, sensation, and a heart capable of gratitude is the most profound and accurate map for a path of fulfillment.

All humans have a natural and organic system of information that moves us around in the world every day, every moment. This system of information is a holistic treasure trove of signals and signs, and it includes an innate propensity to seek completion, accept transition, and heal what hinders its greatest function—our bodies. Our bodies are great transmitters of what is true inside us. Our bodies, with all their unfathomable functioning—the flow of breath and blood, the form of bone, the swell of sensations, feelings, and emotions, meridians and energy systems, mind

41

and spirit, are whole organisms that feed our views and experiences, and they respond to everything.

So much of this system is unconscious and processes all sorts of stimuli quite brilliantly without us having to think about it at all. If we try to "figure things out," with no pause to listen to what is happening internally or to wonder about what wants to happen naturally, we stifle our authentic and essential tendency toward truth and love. The crocus does not say, "Shall I pop up here or there? What if there's a rock in the way, and what if an animal passes that spot or wouldn't it be better if I just waited a few more days?" A grove of aspen does not try to figure out when it should turn gold and orange in the Colorado autumn or whether it's a good idea to provide a canopy for the elk calves in spring. The natural world allows its burgeoning to simply be what, how, and where it is, just as it is. We are made of this nature, as well, until our personalities and egos get in the way.

Appreciation

When we review the course of our lives with an open mind and heart, with a commitment to removing our blinders, we can see that the purpose of all the cycles of changes and endings is to create new growth, a new path in life. Notice where the flow is dammed up in your life and you'll discover where you may have blocks or resistance to change. For example, notice what you complain about the most. Complaining is a major way to fuel resistance and to be run by the ordinary side of self, which is ego or personality. Complaining not only increases our suffering; it is also unpleasant for those around. When you find yourself complaining about someone, ask yourself if this thing you complain about in another person is something you ever do. Your complaint also pulls the shade down on anything that has pleasure and joy in it, right there in that moment. You have the power to create a shift whenever you are willing to catch yourself in the muck of complaining. Again, this is about a conscious choice to shift. Let's look more closely at how to follow the flow.

One primary shift technique is to pause and breathe, notice. Are you aware of the effect your complaint is having on others around you? Notice what you're experiencing in your body. Are you enjoying yourself? Not likely. So how do you want to feel? Look around you for something that ignites your pleasure. It could be the tiniest of things: A nearby flower, a child laughing, the color of the sky, the aroma of coffee in the café where you sit, the recollection of your child's hug that morning. It could be something within you, or even on you, such as appreciating how good you feel in the sweater you chose to wear that day. Continue to breathe slowly and low into your soft belly. That moment's pause and breath can offer the restful ease of appreciation. And there it is. Appreciation!

Let's anchor the sense of appreciation: You begin with a new or renewed commitment and intention to catch yourself in whatever form of resistance you are experiencing. At the moment we're looking at complaining. You catch yourself, or perhaps someone points out to you that you are complaining. Pause, breathe, notice, and ask yourself what you are feeling in that moment. Here's a hint: If you are speaking or thinking in the second or third person— "You did such and so," or "He said this" or "She said that"—you may be complaining. When you shift to thinking or speaking in first person, the language of responsibility, "I feel . . . ," then you are getting to the truth of your own feeling experience.

Once you have acknowledged and tended the real feeling, then find something that generates feelings of pleasure and appreciation. You can find this in your environment or in a body sensation or from an inner resource. The more you practice this, the more it becomes you, a remembered and natural part of you. This creates energy and openness for greater fluidity in your body, emotions, in your day, and within your relationships.

The Body's Vocabulary

Here is a list of descriptive words to play with in your vocabulary. Listen for how they might feel inside you. I'm suggesting that your body has a voice, offering you true signs of what you are feeling and sensing. This is a list of words for your body vocabulary. Become familiar with these and you will increase and enhance your sensory acuity. Please feel free to see this as a place from which to launch your own list. Add your own words that pop up if they feel more suited to you. Listen for what rings true from your body voice.

৯ৎ ৯ৎ ৯ৎ

able dense gristly loose niggling absent drippy juicy grainy lame nagging achy dark gray lumpy frosty nasty biting dicey groovy leaning open flipping bouncy wavy eager icy melting piercing wiry bristly energy lazy scorched crusty touchy pinching brittle ease itchy round super mending parched broken wild zany massive zapped empty full silly pang bubbly masking noisy slippery sweaty heated limber pinging mired pinched bumpy effervescent prancing hovering jammed

*undulating buoyant dazzled yowling heavy feverish
cranky gripped gripping jarred crunchy soft fiery
jangled stiff feisty jumbled prattling rubbery rickety
roaring ratcheted scrunched scraped sick sour
tired vibrant tight tangled tough teasing tingly
twirling tugging sparkly splashing viscous vibrating
windy wishy-washy wary wobbly yawning yanking
whiney wired weary zingy zippy zipped*

You'll find some suggestions for how to play with these words in the Soul Play exercises in Part III. As you listen to the messages your body provides and stretch your body vocabulary, you will grow toward a sense of being at home in yourself. Allow your body to be the ally it naturally is.

Emotional Body

We are also made up of a body of feelings and emotions. This can include everything from a hunch or gut feeling to feeling passionate toward a lover, to feeling impassioned by a muse, to the sensation of awe and quickening at the view of the sunset. This is what I'm referring to as the emotional body.

In the mid 1980s I was involved in a rigorous recovery program for drug and alcohol addiction. The program provided participants with what it called the basic seven, a list of what they considered the basic feelings. Those were: joy, sadness, fear, anger, guilt, love, hate. As you might imagine, most people who were going through such a recovery process were grappling with experiences of guilt, fear, and hate. Developing an understanding of these basic feelings was highly beneficial, and I found it of great service at the time. For now, I'm going to drop the guilt, hate, and love to reveal the primary emotions that I've borrowed from the teachings of Drs. Gay and Katie Hendricks. If you want to expand your emotional awareness, explore and play with identifying these primary feelings: joy, sadness, fear, anger, and sexual feelings. (Love and hate are deep, experiential states that are responsive— or reactive—to combinations of the primary feelings.)

There are innumerable derivatives under each of these basic feelings, some of which are in the body vocabulary list above. Let's add a few more to each of these emotions.

- ✤ Joy—Delight, glee, giddiness, excitement, happiness, flow, love, elation, lightness, energy, and ease.
- ✤ Sadness—Sorrow, grief, bewilderment, low, weepy, regrets.
- ✤ Fear—Scared, jittery, nervous, concerned, anxious, and ambivalent.
- ✤ Anger—Annoyed, irritated, frustrated, tense, resentful, and hateful.
- ✤ Sexual Feelings—warm, hot, charged, passionate, aroused.

Feeling sexual is a territory of its own. Feelings and sensations will depend on many things such as gender or gender identification, where we are, who we're with, the surroundings or environment, and so on. Look at the body vocabulary to assist in naming the vast palate of feelings that emerge as sexual feelings. Notice that sexual feelings can include experiences from each of the other four emotions—for example, warm, hot, charged, passionate, aroused, wet. How about desire, hunger, lust, love, sweaty, tingly, excited, sated, anticipating, flowing. As with the other primary emotions, sexual feelings can emerge anytime and anywhere. All emotions are organic and human, letting you know that you are alive and vibrant. Having sexual or sensual feelings happens within you and requires no object of desire. The more you can become self-referenced about what's happening in your physical and emotional body, as opposed to externally referenced—that is, making it be about someone or something outside of you—the more refined you will be at owning your own experience. Self-referencing expands your capacity to be present and in your integrity.

Now ask yourself what you are feeling in this moment by identifying a primary emotion; then add a word or two describing your body sensation and where in your body you feel that sensation.

_____

_____

_____

_____

_____

_____

_____

It is a powerful inner resource to be able to identify what you are truly feeling, feel it fully, and have a keen understanding of what your body sensation is communicating about your emotions. Refining this emotional skill level will assist you as you move about your day, from one transition to the next. This inner resource enhances connection with self and others, contributing to self-trust, self-esteem, and personal integrity. If our aim is to live in a state of completion and to be open to new beginnings, we'll be more present for them with this inner awareness of our emotional and physical bodies.

We Start at the End

How often do you find yourself beginning at an end—the end of a relationship, end of a project, your kids leaving for college, the end of your workday? Perhaps you've chosen to read this book as you come toward the end of your life. Doesn't it ring true that for so many of life's endeavors, we see that the stepping off point is at the juncture when something else is closing? With any ending there is a beginning and perhaps some release at the start of something new. If we look at this holistically, or shall we say with quantum thought, there is of course, no beginning, no ending. We are in an ever-flowing soul journey, an abundant series of human experiences in which all things, all junctures, have purpose in our lives. In the natural flow of the universe, change is constant.

In the middle of writing this book, as synchronicity would have it, I came across this quote:

> *What we call the beginning*
> *is often the end.*
> *And to make an end*
> *is to make a beginning.*
> *The end is where we start from.*
>
>
>
> *T.S. Eliot*

The Service of Completion

What is it to be "of service"? Can you always tell when something is of service to you?

When I think of myself as being of service, certain qualities need to be present. For one thing, I intend to come into particular events, situations, and interactions with presence and awareness. I also want to meet each circumstance with openness to discovery. So, of course, there are always surprises. There is no way for us to know what is around the corner or who's going to be there or what opportunity awaits our attention. I hold an intention to be open in myself, to be willing, flexible. Commitment, intention to that level of presence and awareness, is like a magnet that draws us back on course when we slip, when we feel defensive, or if awareness simply goes dim. Part of being in what the Buddhists call "right action" or "right relations" is having the consciousness to recognize when we have slipped off course. The Greek etymology "to sin" is literally "to miss the mark." I've slipped, tripped, and fallen flat on my face. I suspect most of us have, and we are likely to again. What I am talking about, then, is something you must truly want for yourself—that is, to intend to create a clear path of awareness and self-responsibility, accountability— happiness.

This requires practice, patience, and self-forgiveness. We will not learn to be more present or honorable by kicking ourselves when we're down. Simply notice. Allow yourself to feel fully what you are experiencing and forgive yourself if you feel you would like to have approached someone or something with greater awareness and integrity. We are allowed to recommit and take responsibility for our missteps. The Six Gates are of service to self and those we encounter.

Imagine for a moment how you might approach your "unfinished business." How might you express your truth such that you come to the end of your day with nothing left unsaid?

_____

_____

_____

_____

_____

_____

Imagine that failure is not possible. Let's say our intentions are pure. That might look like this: No interest in harm to self or other, no attachment to outcome, trust that anything that takes place is only opportunity for learning and increasing awareness and consciousness, an openness to discovery, no expectation that we are to be given something in return for our gesture or intention of completion. Throw in that the heart is truly open to feeling a sense of compassion for self and others. This clarity of intention, of course, increases our chances of coming through the situation peacefully.

Service may imbue a quality of ceremony, nurturance, or even duty. True service has no "what's in it for me?" energy. If you come to the end of an encounter, a meeting, your day, a relationship, a project with any bitterness, angst, or resentment, you have likely not acknowledged or expressed what is fully your truth. Acts of compassion and service are fluid and free processes that ultimately grant all parties a deeper gift of potential, which in turn bestows on us that quickened energy toward creativity, love, and consciousness.

I'm reminded of a particular scene from the movie *Field of Dreams* when Kevin Costner's character, Ray Kinsella, has built the baseball field, watched the games, but now wants to walk into the cornfield.

We're made to imagine this cornfield is heaven. Shoeless Joe Jackson tells him not to go.

"I never once asked what's in it for me!" Ray barks.

"What do you want?" Joe replies.

"Uh, what's in it for me?"

"If you build it, he will come," Joe directs his statement home.

Ray turns to find that it is his father at home base, young and in catcher regalia. This beautiful movie is a fine portrayal of completion. Sometimes we do not start out with the awareness that we are being of service. Costner's character gets it on some level that he is of service throughout his journey and in building the baseball field. But he also forgets it. He becomes attached. There was a deep sense of incompletion between him and his father, regret and unspoken truths. When he sees his father, he suddenly sees the whole purpose, how his choices were of service to his father and the other players.

Completion abounds. It served his own sense of completion in the end, as well.

Wonder if you have come through a certain situation feeling satisfied, feeling acceptance. This isn't to say that whenever we come to a sense of feeling complete, we will be utterly free of feeling any degree of sorrow or fear, of what's next, of the unknown, maybe. Tune into the twinge of angst, frustration, aches, fatigue to find out if you have withheld something.

Imagine the service, then, to self, to family, to community if we were to truly face what feels undone, incomplete, in our lives. We could embrace within ourselves such benefits as space, time, energy, peace, empowerment, forgiveness, freedom, acceptance, quiet, permission, creative flow, joy, connection, rest, sexual aliveness, a deeper sense of integrity, love — just to name a few possibilities.

Another superb ingredient for service is to release any attachment to someone being right and someone being wrong. This has been a freeing formula for my mind and heart when I have felt troubled, or in some relationship jangle. Freeing myself from positioning myself and another person to one side or another has allowed me to create deeper connection, made way for a free flow of forgiveness and communication. This increases the possibility of responsibility, not blame or fault, resting in all the appropriate places for all the participants.

On Your Own

It is true that we will come across certain situations and individuals that, for myriad reasons, will not or cannot show up for an interaction of completion. In other words, we may have prepared ourselves, done an inventory, and are ready to attend to a certain incompletion with another in our life. It is still possible for us to come to a place of resolve even if we invite a person, or perhaps a group of people, to engage in an interaction with the intent to get complete and move on, and they do not respond or they still feel bitter, rejecting the invitation.

Free flow of forgiveness does not require the other person to even be involved in the process. The experience of rejection, resistance, or refusal may also serve us in some way if we are paying attention to our own sense of the impeccability of our intention. If the person with whom we wish to have completion has died, for example, the possibility of making peace is still ours and requires the completion journey to be more inward. The opportunity to open the flow of expression that can ripple outward in service to others remains possible.

I've had the privilege of working as a psychotherapist for more than two decades. I have been blessed with countless, invaluable learning opportunities as a professional and in my personal growth, on every level. Over the last 18 years my interests, both personally and professionally, made a dynamic shift to the more holistic, somatic, and spiritually oriented approaches to healing and raising consciousness. My work with my clients and students is such a rich landscape. My personal life experiences have been the best laboratory in which to first test what I offer in my work. This lab yields one lesson and opportunity after another, to look at myself and wonder if I've come through each encounter, each commitment, conversation, task with a sense of ease.

I've made a commitment to live my life in what I first heard Drs. Gay and Kathlyn Hendricks call a "state of completion," which means that I've also made many other commitments, such as being honest, taking responsibility for my actions, tuning in to my authentic feelings and to healthy communication.

Entanglements

Entanglements in our lives can show us our incompletions, and entanglements can take many forms. For example, the entanglement can be in the form of physical things we hang onto, or we can become entangled with people in our various relationships. Most of us want so much to hang onto things the way they are, even when we don't like the way things are. Whether we are talking about dynamics between people, routines or ruts, or physical things, it is of great service to disentangle.

Let's talk about those physical things we own. When I say things, I mean the things we hang onto. We have cupboards, garages, store rooms, bins, and closets full of college papers, grandmother's cups, old T-shirts, toys, books, broken telephones, Christmas lights that half light up, a carpet sample, unopened boxes left untouched for years. Take a few moments to try on these questions:

What sorts of items are you hanging onto?

_____

_____

_____

_____

_____

_____

_____

What's the "just in case" you are telling yourself about these things?

_____

_____

_____

_____

Are these items keeping you entangled or attached to
something, someone, or some time from your past?

_____

_____

_____

_____

_____

_____

You might want to ask a buddy or even a
professional organizer to assist you in sorting through
these items. As you ask these questions, "What's my
just in case and is there an entanglement here?" notice
what's happening in your body and breath. Listen to
whether there is excitement, easy flow of your breath,
heart opening. Or do you experience your heart pulling

down over an item given to you by a lost love or family member, the constraint of "I really should hang onto this?" It's also possible you really don't know.

Create piles: to the dump, to recycling, for donation, and I-don't-know-yet. I suggest you give yourself a timeframe on the I-don't-know pile, one month perhaps or two. Then that pile goes to the other piles. This process will likely have profound information about you and how you may be contracted in yourself by hanging on to the stuff. Consider that the stuff, piles, things you've stored and haven't worn or touched for years, are all a reflection of what is storing up inside you—inside your body, mind, heart, spirit. Imagine the spaciousness you would create to get current and clear away what is no longer of use to you and may be of better use to others. The external environment, of our own making, is a reflection of what is happening, or maybe not happening, internally. Let yourself celebrate the clearing inside your mind and body when you create more space for living in the now and for your creative expression.

Many people also hang onto relationships long after they cease being a loving vessel where people thrive and grow. I've heard statements such as, "I need to play it safe," or "I don't want to rock the boat." Other very common expressions I've heard are "Oh, I'm used to it" and "It's OK—I can do it."Or "this is just how it is—I'll get by." Some cling to the relationship, or an idea of the potential of it, when it has become wrought with abuse or addiction. Some stay more out of a sense of obligation than something that they feel in their hearts. I recognize this is dicey territory. We may ask "Well, what about the commitment?" Or we may be thinking: "But there's the house, the money, the kids, the trip we already paid for and haven't gone on yet, his promises . . . " Do you trust for certain that your choices are led from your heart? Ask yourself these questions: Are your actions based on what you feel to be true in your heart and body? Or are you led by an internal voice saying, "You should do this or else"? Is there something else that influences your choices?

The "something else" could be the myriad consequences you tell yourself will happen, when in fact you cannot know for sure. Consider that the most serious consequence of all is the breach of your own integrity. Such a breach can create a sense of loss of yourself as a contributing member of your family and community. To have a breach of integrity creates a leak of the feeling of aliveness. We attach to our beliefs, patterns, and judgments. We hold on to hope of understanding what it's all about, trying to figure it out, sometimes desperate to "go back to the way it was." Well, there is no going back. Chances are that "going back" would mean "back to sleep," back into the illusion or denial that created the stuck-ness or unhappiness to begin with.

When you have faced fully into the conflicts that have felt dark or disheartening to you, when you have called on your inner and external resources to assist you in creating the positive steps to mend a life situation, yet you keep hitting a wall—then it's time to begin the steps of completion. It's possible that you are recycling a pattern that returns you to an impasse. Yes, we recycle patterns. Ideally you are looking for ways to create shifts sooner rather than later. Look for how the pattern unfurls differently because you brought greater awareness and integrity to the process. If you are seeing a repetitive pattern that seems the same or feels even worse than before, this might be a state of limbo that sorely needs your commitment to take bigger steps toward change. I do not suggest that you merely jump ship. I encourage you to see the junctures and jangles where you are feeling incomplete. See where you can be fully expressive with yourself as well as with others. These tangled places offer a great opportunity for you to discover how you might best step into what you dearly want for yourself and your relationships.

As you create a conscious shift and stoke the embers of your courage and responsibility to be proactive in your healing and acceptance, you create momentum through your suffering. When you truly take pause and tune into acceptance, you will have a sense of moving forward.

Life wants us to discover itself.
Individuals explore and systems
emerge. They self-transcend into new
forms of being. Newness appears
out of nowhere. We can never predict
what will emerge. We can never
go back. Life is on a one-way street
to novelty. Life always surprises us.

๛

Margaret J. Wheatley
& Myron Kellner-Rogers
A Simpler Way

You may find yourself resisting or refusing to move forward. You may feel deeply hurt, wounded, betrayed by an event, a colleague, friend, community or group, your church, parent or other family member, your child, or former love. It can be very difficult to recognize how holding someone to blame is an imprisonment of the blamer. Such posturing holds one captive from truly being here now and living life in the present—mind, heart, and body. It may be even more of a stretch to acknowledge that whatever event we resist accepting or resent from our past, may actually have been a gift to us in some way.

The way to look deeper is to wonder what is keeping us from being fully in our life in the present, not to revisit the past in such a way as to hold us hostage somewhere in 1952 or 1967 or last year. It is neither fun nor interesting nor beneficial to chisel away at the details of past events that wounded us. I am suggesting a more responsible trip, an exploration of what is happening inside us at this moment that may be influenced by a pocket of unfinished, unexpressed truth from the past. The journey through *The Six Gates of Completion* and honest self-inquiry as you play with the exercises in Part III are how you creatively discover the untold and unmet expression from the past.

Listening for What You Want

Your body speaks. Listening to your body-voice will serve you, and ultimately others, in creating more flow and connection and less drama in your interactions.

Some of us learned how to discern what we feel emotionally or physically by noticing what we are not feeling. Here is a thumbnail sketch of how this tuning in could look:

BJ: So what do you notice feeling right now, as you are telling me that?

Client: Well, I don't know—I feel OK [or good/fine/nothing really/I don't know].

BJ: And what do you notice about what "OK" feels like in your body? Where is OK located in your body?

Client: Uh—in my body—well, I'm not feeling tense, not anxious or anything.

BJ: Let yourself take another deep breath and send the breath low into your belly. So where do you notice you are not feeling tension? (I encourage soft belly breathing, in through the nose and out through the nose.)

Client: Hmmm—my shoulders.

BJ: And if you are noticing your shoulders and they are not feeling tension, what are they feeling?

Client: Oh—hmmm—well, my shoulders feel relaxed, they've dropped.

If you are struggling to find out what you are feeling, first notice the struggle. There are likely some feelings and sensations that accompany any effort or struggle to discover what you are experiencing first. That may be the first layer to get through. Gently breathe with a soft belly, breathe slowly into your tummy. Pause and wonder to yourself. If you are still unsure about what you are feeling, notice what is not there in your shoulders, your gut, forehead, lower back, jaw, eyes, pelvis, your heart or chest. You may have an awareness of a chill on your neck, or your feet are warm, for instance. There is so much your body is experiencing all the time. It is important to notice those sensations and bring them into your awareness, maybe even speaking them out loud. And notice your breath. Simply come back again to the gentle flow in through your nose, out through your nose. Just notice without judging your experience. Sometimes simply noticing can shift an uncomfortable feeling experience into one that has more energy and clarity.

You can use this process to look into what is of service to you and how you are of service. I invite you to wonder into this as a stepping stone for accepting the service of completion. You might want to have a completion with or about a particular person who is unavailable to you—for example, if the person has died. You can still engage in active steps to come to a state of completion. Some of the exercises in Part III will assist in that type of completion process.

Let Go of the Outcome

For all our good intentions, there is no way for us to know just how things will unfold. Clinging to any expectation for something to turn out in a particular way is not the best idea. Certainly we have heard this from many great teachers of spirituality, meditation, Eastern religions, and psychology, who tell us to release expectation, let go of attachment, eliminate the need to understand, let go of the outcome. I've found myself mightily frustrated with such advice many times. I've also found that with practice, yielding to what is has given me more ease and flow toward completion. Letting go of the outcome while holding a heartfelt intention, having goals, a well-laid plan, along with action steps toward a desired result, are all fine ingredients for creating a pleasurable sense of resolution. Again, for all our well-laid plans, there is no way for us to know just how things will unfold.

When I first started writing this book, I had an initial and vague course of action, like determining what to put in the introduction and what would go in Part II. I found out quickly that to make way for my creative energy and allow for its fluidity, I needed to simply write, letting the process be more abstract. I'll know where it is all supposed to go when the time is right. As I write now, in this moment, my plan is to complete this book. I am committed to completing the writing of this book. I have a vision of what the tangible outcome might be, and as I feel into that, I experience a quickening and joy, a sense of expansion about it. For this moment, I am not feeling attached to just how it will turn out. I have no understanding of all that I will learn to get this project to be a book on the bookstore shelves and into your hands to read. And so, with no expectation of the outcome in this moment—given that you are reading my process—my project of writing this book will have been successful, completed.

How does one let go of the outcome? A fine and tricky question, indeed. To evoke an answer to how, we must first be committed to what. Whether it is to a plan, a project, an intention, a person, it is commitment that leads to how. Hold an intention in your mind and in your heart. Allow yourself to be open to discovery. Make clear agreements with yourself and with others on what action to take. Giving your attention to these steps is what I have found to be most effective. I think of particular teachers who have helped me to integrate and refine these steps, and I feel my gratitude for them regularly.

When we offer others what we want, such as love, generosity, forgiveness, patience, attention, we open more space to receive it ourselves.

You must be the change you wish to see in the world.

ও

Mahatma Gandhi

A key element to add is giving to someone what you want for yourself. This practice of holding for another or giving to another that which you want to bring to yourself increases the sense of fulfillment within yourself. For example, if you want forgiveness from someone, hold that state of forgiveness for yourself and for the other. If it is connection, attention, space—give these to yourself first and then to the other. If you find yourself frustrated, put out, or saddened that something or someone "out there" is not giving you what you want or what you expected, ask yourself if you are giving that to yourself and to others. Have you worked through and tended all the feelings that are rumbling in you regarding a situation? Are you simply expecting the other person to get through their feelings first and get over it? Are you feeling disrespected, for instance? If so, this would be a good time to ask yourself how you exude the quality of respect. Are you being respectful to others? Do you see and treat yourself respectfully? Is the response you are receiving from others directly or indirectly an invitation for you to wonder on what qualities you are generating within yourself and in your own attitudes and behaviors? In the same vein, are you feeling heard? If not, it's a good time to wonder how you might be listening to yourself or listening to others more deeply, actively. Putting our attention on what we truly wish to create will expand that energy and increase our potential for creating it.

In-Between

Everything requires space and time to gestate properly. You have conceived ideas and plans, projects to be created. After a certain period of gestation something shifts, the birth of yet another idea or the manifestation of a new job or piece of music or a conversation with a friend. The unknown undulates between and beneath all the great beginnings and endings of our lives.

There is such a play of opposites in the in-between places of our lives. The junctures, crossroads, the end-of-this and not-yet-that places are those liminal phases in our lives that contain a mystery. This place of mystery is fertile and creative ground to explore ourselves more deeply. These transitional places in life tend to be the very spots most of us either fear greatly or prefer to avoid altogether. I encourage you to step right into the void and take these offerings with you: this book and others; a list of whom to call if life feels too shaky; music for the journey; a teacher or witness; a commitment to self-care (eating well, drinking water, scheduling a massage, planning to talk or sit with your teacher or friend).

In the early stages of waking from my addiction, I was given a powerful insight: When you're in an experience of letting go of one trapeze bar and not yet grasping the next, this mid air (in-between) place is where we are most alive. I do not recall the source, but I have found it profoundly useful and have reaped from its simple wisdom often. (Addiction, by the way, is one form of resisting the void while in it, and recovery can feel like deliberately stepping straight into the void.)

Another similar gift I've heard is that music happens between the notes and is most resonant in the rests. The music is still alive and vibrant even in the pauses. Hearing is a process that takes place within the ear because of space, a passageway, a portal through which air passes to tap the drum, thereby making sound. Imagine that: a portal, open space, air carrying the frequencies through to the brain. If the way is blocked somehow, the sound is either distorted or inaudible or even painful.

The Buddhist tradition provides a profound example of these in-between places. Buddhists believe that when one dies, the soul does not leave the body immediately. It enters a transitory phase, having departed this human form while traversing to whatever comes next: the next life or perhaps ultimate enlightenment. Tibetan Buddhists honor ancient practices by wrapping the body in a particular way, chanting over the departed, anointing them, saying mantras to banish any karma or darkness that would hinder their journey, praying for their safe passage.

This is done for many days before the loved one is carried in procession to the cremation pyre. There is no sense of finality in death, no end, but an abiding faith that the soul moves on to attain dharma. The soul never dies.

There is a distinction here between transition and limbo. Transition is an organic and necessary crossroad, a liminal phase where we simply surrender to the waves of change. We must allow the transition to take its own time. Where transition is movement, limbo is an inability to move, it's a place of not choosing, of hanging onto the one trapeze bar until it is too late to reach for another. You have missed your chance, at least this one. Some other choice will arise, to be sure. Another opportunity for actively choosing the journey toward completion is inevitably right in front of you.

Tools for the Soul

Transitions and losses can direct us to live life from the heart, with greater intimacy and consciousness.

Change can happen quickly, and sometimes we take a leap of faith, swinging ourselves out and into the void and then surrendering to it, not knowing what's on the other end of the transition. You have the potential to find the sweetest of pearls to enrich your soul in these times of great change. There are many tools and resources available to assist in excavating the pearls of wisdom.

One tool for the soul's journey is the Tarot deck. The Tarot is a pack of 78 cards, each card a guide on your spiritual journey. For example, the Fool is the first card in the Major Arcana (a division of the Tarot deck). Because it is the first, it is given the number zero. Beginning in nothingness, the Fool's journey—launched from the state of utter emptiness, mystery, and space—holds the free spirit of hopefulness, openness, freedom, and possibility. It is from this place—the void—where we can make enormous life-changing decisions that may feel ludicrous to us or will seem so to others.

---

*Mystical consciousness allows you to view
the trauma of a job loss or divorce
as a new beginning. You can see
that you have been forced to grow out of
a symbolic cocoon and made to change into
something new. Certain life changes are, in fact,
altars of transformation. Mystical consciousness
can give you the grace to illuminate
your every moment, not just the difficult ones.*

Caroline Myss
Entering the Castle—An Inner Path to God
and Your Soul

Another example from the Tarot is the Tower card, which makes most of us say "Uh-oh" when we turn it over in a reading: The Tower represents destruction of old ways and patterns. Its message is primarily that life as you have known it is about to tumble into mere bits and it is time to wonder what is crucial for you to salvage. Otherwise, let it all go and make your choices about what most wants to rise from the ashes—in short, what do you want to create next? Your very worldview is being altered when you are in the place of the Tower. It is an organic unfolding of destruction, creation, gestation.

I've discovered that turning Tarot cards is a way of tuning even further inward, accessing my inner teacher, or my witness self. It is not about taking the Tarot so literally that you remove yourself from a natural process through an issue or life events. It is useful to allow the images and messages of the Tarot to serve as guideposts, just as you might use your own dreams. My experience is that my inner teacher, my intuition, may want an extra stir of inspiration from time to time. It can be helpful to meditate on the Tarot as it pertains to your current circumstances or question. The Tarot is a good resource for adjusting your inner awareness dial.

I imagine you have often heard the reference to the transmutation of the caterpillar into the butterfly as a metamorphosis, a strange and remarkable force of nature. What you may not know, however, is that the cocoon is not at all a lovely resting place. I once enjoyed the notion of the cocoon as a warm and cozy comforting place to hunker down and be restored. In fact, the cocoon contains a goopy, slimy mess made of the death of the caterpillar. The slimy substance of that death is the very material that supports the growth of new life. Metaphoric metamorphosis is the same journey, don't you think? Something in or around us is dying and may feel goopy and slimy during the process of rebirth.

Ideally, each time you allow yourself to yield to this uncomfortable and transitional phase of your journey, more of you is born. Your soul is making its way beyond your ego. Your heart becomes the leader of your ways and decisions. The Divine expresses itself through that innate spark that is your essence. It is your essence, your authentic self, that yearns to shine through the mists of what you told yourself and others about who you are. My understanding is that the Divine, or Love, or Spirit, or God, is you and is me. So wouldn't it be the loving and responsible path to allow the Divine to express Itself through the clear portal of your authentic and essential self? For me, the answer is a resounding yes! This is a practice—practice experiencing and expressing who you truly are.

What is limbo then? Limbo has the elements and sensations of resistance, broken agreements, rationalizing rather than truly listening to the tone of the heart. Limbo has a different feeling quality and texture in both mind and body. Truly letting go, surrendering into the mystery, feels quite different from citing the reasons for leaving that or starting this. Yielding to the gestational phase of something certainly does not mean that nothing is happening. On the contrary, it means that you will free yourself from the habit of trying to figure it out. If you are saying, for instance, "I've just got to figure this out," or "I'm trying so hard but I just don't get why he/she_____," you are in a state of resistance. You are actively pushing away the very hope of peace or resolve you wish to attain.

We humans naturally want to understand. We want to understand why things are the way they are, how things work. Don't we often discover that no matter how much we have come to understand, everything eventually changes? It is our openness to discovery, not clutching to understand, that allows learning and creativity to emerge. If we attach to things staying the same, there is no fluidity or space for us to swim in the vast ocean of creative flow and a world of discovery.

Making clear commitments, knowing what agreements you want to make or need to shift, being impeccably truthful with yourself and others—these are primary ingredients for the most restorative and nourishing aspects of life and its endless tides of change.

If we find ourselves in doubt that we're up to being a warrior-in-training, we can contemplate this question: "Do I prefer to grow up and relate to life directly, or do I choose to live and die in fear?"

ও

Pema Chodron
Comfortable with Uncertainty

As an American Buddhist nun, Pema Chodron, author of *Comfortable With Uncertainty*, *The Places That Scare You*, and *When Things Fall Apart*, offers a pure, direct, and accessible approach to Buddhist tradition. In *Comfortable With Uncertainty*, when she speaks of the "warrior-in-training," she is referring to warriors of compassion: ". . . not warriors who kill but warriors of nonaggression who hear the cries of the world." She calls us to bring this open, compassionate part of ourselves to the foreground, setting aside our reactivity. "A warrior accepts that we can never know what will happen to us next . . .we can never avoid uncertainty."

My experience is that my own suffering has been amplified by my non-acceptance of change, mystery, impermanence. As I practice what I am offering to you and what other wise and beloved teachers offer to us, I have grown to be more of a witness to my own process. An increased capacity to see and respond with less illusion of control and enhanced capacity for being open with compassion can be yours, too. I no longer drift toward the habit of adding to my suffering by being attached to how things should have turned out. My suffering has decreased or even been nonexistent in certain experiences because I am now less shocked by the transitions and growth spurts, changes and endings that are inevitable and out of the realm of control.

Many of us enjoy the element of surprise: the kind of surprise where something pops into our energy field and awareness, a light bulb goes off and we make a discovery. Play with the energy and surrender in acceptance. Let yourself have the flow of feelings, as well.

To accept also means you are accepting feelings flowing through, tears running down your face, uncertainty bringing in the fog. Let it be. It will change. The feeling will shift at some point as you allow yourself the space you need for expression. I have worked with many people who have feared they would never stop crying if they let the dam break. Contracting around a wound causes further pain and suffering when what the wound needs is the salve of tears to heal. Sometimes it only takes a moment of breath and tender attention and permission for the feeling to emerge and to be felt so that years of holding back can be released. I've never yet met anyone who didn't have some other feeling emerge after a while: an exhale followed by freed-up energy, a settling in and settling down, a sense of rest, tensions released; then another wave of different feelings rises up, thoughts of appreciation, thoughts of being free.

We sometimes have to ride many waves of feeling to gain greater clarity.

The one thing that remains the same
is that nothing remains the same.
As we accept and acknowledge life's passing nature,
we are freed to cherish the moments that pass
in bittersweet glory. No matter how difficult,
life is beautiful. No matter how beautiful,
life is difficult.
This is the great paradox that opens the heart
and brings compassion. We are all travelers
on the vast and shifting sands of time.
We are all inconsequential and important,
very small and very large. Our transitions are like
octaves building brilliantly upon each other.
We are life's music, so let us dance.

Julia Cameron
Transitions—Prayers and Declarations
for a Changing Life

From Grief to Celebration

We are likely to go through a multitude of changes and transitions without even noticing. When we pay attention, feelings arise. The great transitions in our lives grant us opportunities to drop into our own depths, opening to grief, fear, compassion, and the ecstatic experience of love. The heart breaks, and that breaking open can feel bone-shaking as something inside dies. I know from my own experience of dying into life that we each have the capacity to move through these experiences, which St. John of the Cross called the Dark Night of the Soul. Stay the course. Seek the witness of a good teacher or wise friend. Do not fight it; face into it. (See the appendix for a list of books that make good companions as we journey through these rites of passage.)

The experience of a "dark night" can be short-lived or can take years to traverse. It can feel like dropping into the depths of a mystery that is riveting, shaky, and uncertain. We tend to want more quiet, rest, solitude. The dark night can feel like an abyss of unending grief and alienation. It can be a murky dense place or a place full of space. I've worked with many people who have journeyed dark nights, and I have experienced my own. The passage through a dark night of the soul has a different texture than having the blues or being in uncertain times.

The nature of this time can feel like a spiritual crisis or existential angst rather than the angst and gyrations of the personality. The best we can do is yield to it. Surrender! Any resistance or efforts to figure it out will increase our suffering and hide those pearls we are meant to find during this profound journey. Seek out a witness to support you in this journey, someone who can be by your side or even a thousand miles away to remind you that you are not alone. Find comfort in the words of wise writers who have journeyed through their own dark nights. Their companionship may even "normalize" what feels like the most unfamiliar territory. The insight and compassion gained by those many others who have traversed this rough terrain can be a comfort to the evolving heart. There is nothing to fix. All that you need to do is be.

Closure Beyond The Loss

The sadness or grief we feel upon the death of a loved one or the end of a relationship that once was dear is the measure of the love we still have flowing in our heart for the other person. The extent of our grief could also be a measure of our wish to feel again their love. Gently wonder as you let yourself find what is true within yourself. Healing from such a deep wound will ultimately be based in love. Suffering is perpetuated by your thoughts, tendrils that twist around the arguable claim of who was right and who was wrong. Maybe you have a story that you cannot come to completion because the person you are grieving over is not here, won't do what you ask, won't talk to you, is dead. Those things may be true.

There are no mistakes in relationships;
everything unfolds the way it's supposed to.
From our first encounter with one another
to our last good-bye, we are in relationships
with each other. We learn through them to see
our souls, with their rich topography, and to
deliver ourselves to healing.
When we let go of our preconceived agendas in loving
relationships, we set aside questions
of whom we will love and for how long.
We transcend these limits to find a love that is magical
and created by a force greater than us,
just for us.

৶

Elizabeth Kubler-Ross
Life Lessons

All kinds of endings and transitions turn and weave through our lives, whether we celebrate them or not. I invite you to celebrate them. As you strengthen your inner witness and notice yourself moving through life transitions, you will find more to celebrate. Honor the fact that you've created a completion, that you've made more space for your energy and concentration. You may find there is more room internally as well as within your environment. Now you can place your attention on creativity, rest, play, contemplation, increased sense of presence and enjoyment with your children and family, patience, forgiveness, health.

A graduate apprentice of the Hendricks Institute Apprentice program expresses his full journey of completion with his father like this:

I was in NYC visiting my Mom for a week. While I was there I had the opportunity to release my Dad's ashes with her. His girlfriend had half of his ashes put aside for me and I still had not requested them from her after two years.

Two years later I was still thinking about how I would dispose of his ashes. I was thinking of wrapping them up in a ball of duct tape and then pounding them with a bat for a while then putting them inside a heavy bag and punching and kicking it until I felt like moving to the next activity, which was putting the ball in the middle of the cul-de-sac I live on and running over it repeatedly with my truck. I was wanting to give him the anger that I still carried about my life with him. I thought to finish by digging a hole at the beach, dumping the ashes in and covering it up. Let the ocean take it all when it might.

I expressed all this to G. in a coaching session. She said get the ashes and do it. If you still feel this way after two years, then do it.

I requested and received my Dad's ashes a month later. Faced with the reality and imminence of my envisioned "program," I realized that I was not separate from my father and that I would really be doing everything that I envisioned to myself. I decided to treat the ashes as if they were my own.

I rode around with the ashes in my car and took scoops full at different times and deposited them at various locations that were meaningful to me, like the beach at sunset and moon rise and at the river mouth at the Esalen Institute in Big Sur. Each time I eulogized myself as I wanted to be eulogized when I died. I talked about my accomplishments and my legacy.

I was ready to be done finally and brought the ashes home with me to NYC where I grew up. I had never envisioned including my mother in the disposal of the ashes until a friend inspired me. My parents hated each other and had a nasty divorce after 44 years of marriage. I realized that my mom needed the closure as much as I. I told my Mom that the closure would liberate her energy still stuck in the relationship. I invited her to contemplate where in her life she would like the liberated energy to go, in support of what she wanted to create in those areas. She thought about it on the drive to the beach.

I went to the place where we all shared the best times together as a family. That area was no longer open beach as it had been reclaimed as a wildlife habitat. We walked on an elevated pathway out into the preserve. At a spot as close as we could get to the historical location of our joyful times together, we each spoke our intentions for the energy we were liberating with the closure of this chapter of life. I felt a heavy sadness in my chest and presented it to my mother. She shared that she felt sad about how difficult the relationship had been for so long.

I feel sad as I recount this story and I also feel so very complete. I am so grateful that I was able to see through all the history and the emotion to a deeper truth and to get to a place where I could create something beautiful and powerful for myself and my Mom. ~ C.H.

This revealing account of completion is one that portrays what I call celebration. It may seem paradoxical to propose celebration and grief as coming from the same well. Willingness to step into the quagmire of grief and all its churning thoughts and sensations is necessary on the journey of completion. Hold the intention of closure, peace, as you ride the waves through bits of content, fragments of stuff that you are willing to release as the truth emerges. Our truth will be found in what we sense and experience in our physical body, as well as within the bell-ringing emotional transparency of our vulnerable self.

Whole Truth—What Does Your Body Say?

When intention comes from that true place of integrity, and when we are in celebration, we become aware of an increased sensory acuity. We're more attuned to our feelings instead of our thoughts. Our deeper sensory awareness allows us the experience and expression of feeling that no one can argue with. These are expressions of one's experience that Dr. Gay Hendricks calls unarguable. For example, "My stomach aches. I'm feeling pressure in my solar plexus. I feel scared/sad/angry/joyful/sexual." These are unarguable statements. Arguable statements sound like this, "You are so cruel and it makes me angry, and not only that, you never listen." The former statements come from our center, a place of responsibility where we embody our own experience: we take ownership of the experience. From this more centered and responsible position, you may be aware of how others or your environment affect you, while also knowing you are in charge of your own experience. The latter statement comes from blame.

Such statements indicate that you have given another person control over what can only be your experience. Arguable statements imply a belief that the one you are blaming has some power over you and that your feelings, maybe even your life, depend on how the other person behaves. In this case, there would be no opening within you to celebrate your own ability to respond, your own responsibility, your own body/mind/emotion/spirit within you, the vessel of your human existence.

Grief is a vast and deep journey that is widely spread throughout our lives. When I say, "From Grief to Celebration," I visualize a spiral, a movement of feelings, layers unfurling one after the next: grief, joy, acceptance, wonder, appreciation, disbelief, grief, ritual, anger, euphoria, peace, grief, creativity, sadness, mystery, celebration—and so on, not necessarily in that order.

One grief stirs another. The experience of a loss, a divorce, a move, the holidays, and even "small" transitions can awaken an old, sleeping giant of grief, perhaps taking us back to the death of a loved one years ago or even decades ago. When we have lost someone we deeply love, someone who is intrinsic to who we are, we are always aware that we are alive and that person is not. This awareness is like a thread woven through the tapestry of the life we had with them and how they remain hidden in the fine fibers of our being long beyond their death.

I know. Every December since I was fifteen, my entire body is fully aware of the smells, energies, songs, and the somatic memory of who was there when my mother died. I have images, a felt sense, memories of the days of the wake, the Catholic ritual of viewing her body, saying goodbye, the quantity and elaborateness of flower arrangements tightly fit into the room, the dress I picked out for her, the Rosary, my own weeping mixed with shock and intense love. The funeral was on Christmas Eve, and I remember staring out the window on the long drive to St. Charles on Long Island where she was buried. I remember and feel it all now, but with more quiet, less sting, more joy, with love as the prevailing tone more than loss. It is as though the trauma and grief of my mother's sudden death have now been soaked in love and celebration—of her, of the holidays she loved so dearly, of the anniversary of her death. This anniversary is a time to love myself, to hold myself tenderly and let the present, my current environment, my family here embrace me and celebrate with me. Part of the celebration is that this life-altering event did not crush me after all. It has chiseled my heart and soul in a manner that feels sacred to me, has refined me and opened me to love and to learn beyond what may have been possible had I not experienced such a loss.

My mother's firstborn, my dear half brother, is a remarkable, generous man, and widely published author of poetry and haiku. Here are two of his poems from his book, *BLOOD (family) AND INK (Poems 1996-2002)* that demonstrate his moving from grief to celebration of our mother.

Mom's Gifts

୬

She gave me the flesh of her flesh, blue eyes,
long legs and my once red hair. She nurtured me
at her breasts, taught me to walk, to swim and tried
to teach me patience

When boys being boys, scrapped and pummeled
or played too rough like tomcats tumbling, she called
on God to give her strength. Yet she often sang so
walls echoed with the sweet soprano of her voice.

At her feet I learned to harvest truth, gather the wisdom
that fell between words, to heal as she tutored me,
with hugs and honeyed tea.

In time, she spoke of music hall dreams and helped
me write my verse. Now "thank you" stands too feeble
a phrase when memory sleeps in stone.

୬

William Scott Galasso

The Passing

ॐ

No caroling this year
where your voice was now
only the wind is heard

ॐ

William Scott Galasso

Grief and celebration, yielding to the river of feelings that stream from and through each of those states, also makes way for gratitude. Gratitude is the element that marries grief and celebration. Coming into a celebratory embodiment of those waves of loss and grief will bring sweetness into the bitter. I see in Scott's poems the sweetness of memory and the appreciation and love he feels for his mother, like the "honeyed tea." While he celebrates and honors her life, he acknowledges his grief with his reference to "sleeping in stone," which I think of as contraction, a moment frozen in time.

The connection we make when we choose the comfort and company of the arts is sweet, clarifying, and touches the soul. Reading or listening to poetry and music through times of transition and grief is a way to affirm for ourselves, and feel affirmed, that what we are experiencing is indeed extraordinary.

PART II:
THE SIX GATES

❧   ❧   ❧

We are drawn by nature toward the desire for completion, just as we are drawn to new beginnings. We have innumerable opportunities to refine the experience of living complete as we meet a host of life transitions and initiations. Part I gave you a glimpse of the every-day incompletions we experience in life; Part II offers a more developed look at completion, what I call the Six Gates of Completion.

- ❧   First Gate ~ Expressing Truth
- ❧   Second Gate ~ Following Through
- ❧   Third Gate ~ Taking True Responsibility
- ❧   Fourth Gate ~ Facing Regrets & Resentments
- ❧   Fifth Gate ~ Tending Remorse
- ❧   Sixth Gate ~ Forgiving

As I have explored and refined this topic for myself, I realize how these key components of completion are best imagined as a tapestry—a harmonious weaving of cooperative elements rather than a linear process. Gates and gateways are metaphors for the portals of growth and clarity we pass through in the process of completion. Release any expectation that the journey of completion should unfold from one stage to the next. We may go through these gates in any way, randomly, in any order, and we may revisit any of them, any time. Each passage fuels and inspires us along the way, through one gate and another.

Photo by BJ Brown

The First Gate:

Expressing the Truth

How do we shift this primary incompletion: important communications that have not been expressed? Expressing the Truth is one gateway we will pass through countless times throughout the rest of our lives. It is a good idea to always keep this gateway open. As we move through the other gates of completion, it is inevitable that we'll keep coming back to this one.

Imagine living life in transparency, which is another way of saying no more secrets, no withholding or finagling the truth, and certainly, no more lies. Pause for a moment and wonder about it. What would it be like to be utterly transparent—at work, at home, in your friendships, and relating with your loved ones? Revealing truth and feelings allows for greater intimacy. It is possible to live this way. Even better, it is most possible to love this way.

In the film *Liar Liar*, Jim Carey plays a slimy lawyer who is suddenly unable to tell lies because of a wish his son made as he blew out the candles on his birthday cake. Carey's character is forced to go through some challenging and amusing gyrations to find out not only *the* truth but *his* truth. You won't need to face the humiliation this fellow endures in the movie. We develop great satisfaction and self-trust as we continue to wonder, intend, and commit to being revealing. I encourage you to practice, and here is a very simple way: Imagine how you would respond to someone asking, "How are you today?" Many people are quick to give pat replies, such as "I'm good" or "Fine" or "OK." The next time you are in a grocery store checkout line and the cashier asks how you are, ask yourself what fine truly means for you in that moment. If you say, "I'm OK," what does OK feel like in your body, in that moment? You are not obliged to explain to the cashier that you are currently feeling irritated because someone got the last gallon of organic milk. You do not have to express your sadness at your child's meltdown that morning, though revealing with a stranger would certainly enhance your experiment. This is an opportunity for you to look at how honest you really are with yourself and with others. You could let the cashier know some real truth beyond your "OK." You might even say, "I'm feeling sad today. Thanks for asking." See it as an experiment that increases your own awareness. Then when you want to express some larger and more significant communication with someone close, you have a greater connection with your inner landscape and the truth of it.

Transparency with loved ones can create a thrumming fear in many people. The emotional stakes are far higher than with someone we do not know. The closer the person is, the more intimate the relationship and the higher the perception of emotional risk or even threat. It is exactly in this context where it is most important to be open and honest. One exception, however, is this: If there is an abusive dynamic present, it is vital that you seek support from someone in whom you feel unwavering trust. The aim is still to communicate fully and authentically. This could be with a family member or friend. Seek guidance from a trusted professional, counselor, or teacher, someone who can help you direct your life toward being free from emotional or physical harm.

I've heard a multitude of reasons why people choose to not express a long withheld and important communication. For example, "Well, it happened so many years ago. It would just hurt him if I told him now" or "I really just want to protect her." "I know she couldn't handle hearing about this." These are rationalizations for not being honest, and they are more about self-protection than protecting another. Underneath, holding the communication back is an attempt at avoiding an undesired reaction.

Our defenses are likely to be triggered when we tell our truth and the person receiving the communication reacts in a way we don't like. Here are a couple of interesting reactions to the other person's reaction when we reveal something: "Well, I'm telling you now!" Or "This is why I didn't want to tell you! I knew you'd freak out." I encourage you to breathe your way through your revealing. Be patient with the other person and with yourself. Your withholding a truth, or telling a lie, can cause great dismay. It boils up a sense of betrayal and sorrow, certainly for the recipient of your breach of trust and likely within you. Go slowly and stay firmly in your intention to create completion, to honor your own integrity, no matter how new to it you may be. Stay on your course and feel your desire for a clean slate.

Ultimately, we free up the flow of energy when we communicate our truth while being sure we are expressing what we are unarguably feeling. Revealing makes way for healthier and more trustworthy expression between speaker and listener. Interest in taking responsibility and being accountable for our own words and deeds is essential here and throughout our quest to live in completion.

Expressing our feelings honestly, revealing what is true, allows us to call ourselves and potentially others to a sense of closure. It also brings us to a threshold. We have a better chance of finding ourselves at a new beginning.

We are influenced not only by the pulls and expectations of our culture but by such contexts as family beliefs, religion, ethnicity, geography. Some people learn to give their power away, controlled by family themes or limiting rules that become the authority in our lives. We take on beliefs that may not only be limiting but also false because of the imprints of our biology and our biography. We might come to believe, for instance, that it is far better to withhold our true feelings so that others will be more comfortable or to avoid expressing the truth so as not to disappoint someone.

Stepping into our own power and self-authority means we are willing to be more truly authentic. A commitment to authenticity strengthens those muscles of self-acceptance and self-respect. When we are integrated in this way, we let go of the "power-over" dynamic. Power over, controlling, coercing, manipulating others, blame, posturing are all based in fear. To be empowered, self-respecting, resting in a place of compassion for self and others, even in the face of adversity—these are rooted in love.

What rings true and feels organic to you is your authenticity. Many years ago, an old friend and teacher pointed out to me that when we're being authentic, it is because our inside and our outside match. Letting the inside and the outside match is a way to be transparent, to live in ourselves, in family, at home and in community where the authentic self can be distinctly seen. Throughout these pages are many examples of authenticity. They all further illustrate living from the inside out.

There is no weapon for the realization
of the truth that is more powerful than this:
to accept yourself.

ॐ

Swami Prajnanpad

Photo by BJ Brown

The Second Gate:
Following Through

The Second Gate is about making clear agreements and making good on unkept promises. Following through also means being honest and communicating with those with whom we wish to create completion. For example, someone may come to you and express their disappointment or hurt that you have broken your promise to pay back a debt. Follow-through is overtly simple here—repay what you owe. The way to follow through fully would be to take responsibility, which means communicating your own recognition, sadness, or fear about not paying up as you agreed. It might sound something like this: "I see that I have not honored our agreement. I recognize I didn't do my part to pay you back when I said I would." Or "I'm sad I didn't take care of that, and I want to now." Another possibility is this: "I appreciate your lending the money. I didn't take care of my part as I agreed. I intend to make and keep clear agreements in the future." Something like this goes quite a distance as you physically make good on the promise (hand over the money, so to speak) and speak sincerely about your responsibility. This is where you leave out the defenses. Extending your gratitude and appreciation for the loan while expressing your unarguable truth about your incompletion is an added clearing of messy energy between you and the other person.

Clear agreements are the agreements we truly want to make and ones that we can keep. Sometimes we gain clarity about our agreements by seeing how an agreement we made is not working or is perhaps detrimental to our own growth in some way. It could be you are unable to follow through on your agreement in a timely fashion for a truly legitimate reason. Perhaps your car broke down as you were on your way to someone's home to follow through on a service you'd agreed to provide. It is still possible to make the call later, indicating your intention to complete the service at another, agreed-upon time.

Whenever we break a promise or don't follow through with an agreement, we create a breach of trust—and a great opportunity to examine how we make agreements. Most people experience a feeling of disappointment over a broken agreement. Most of us know the piercing sting of a broken heart or a betrayal. The greatest healing occurs when we look at ourselves with compassion.

Ask yourself if an agreement you made with someone is a clear agreement. Were there points along the way—through the project, throughout the relationship—when some communication or shift in the agreement needed to occur but didn't? For example, a woman came to a student of mine and requested they barter services with one another. Each one has skills the other sought. The woman made a clear request of my student to provide a particular service within a week. Let's call my student Dee and the other Pam. Dee said she'd like to do this exchange, agreed that she would, and followed through within the requested time. Dee requested of Pam a reciprocated task, and Pam agreed. They did not, however, have a clearly stated amount of time in which Pam's service would be delivered. As time passed, Dee would send Pam an occasional email saying such things as "Hey, how's that project going? I'm excited to get it." Though Dee interacted with Pam on several occasions, she repeatedly missed the opportunity to state clearly what she wanted and did not make a clear request about when she'd like to receive Pam's service. Eight months later, Dee was still waiting—and feeling resentment. Initially, it looked like Pam was wishy-washy with her agreement. Dee felt sad at the discovery that she did not follow through for herself.

To clarify the steps for Dee: She has discovered her true feelings (evoked by Pam's delay, a lesson in disguise). Dee now has the opportunity to explore exactly what she wants. (It is important to ask yourself what you truly want.) Once Dee became clear about what she really wanted, she could finally communicate that to Pam. Dee has opened several gateways here. As you'll see later in this chapter, Dee traverses the fourth gateway as her feelings emerge and she faces her own resentment. She stepped into her true responsibility in the scenario—third gateway. She also brought herself to a new commitment to follow through, make good on the promise—second gateway. Expressing her truth to Pam was the next profound step for her. Dee directly communicated how she felt—first gateway. She became accountable for her own experience and made a clear request for what she wanted from Pam and by when. By understanding that the subtle nudges she made to Pam were unclear communications, Dee was able to empower herself. This made it possible for her to stand up for herself and "close the gap."

Closing the gap is the ability to express the truth and actively create a shift toward what we want, as close to the moment of the event as possible. What I foresee for Dee is that she will continue to close the gap now, sooner rather than later, by clearly communicating what she wants and when she wants it.

There are promises and commitments that carry a deeper emotional thread throughout relationships. Where there is a betrayal of a more intimate nature between people, the breach of trust can sting to the core and permeate the consciousness of both people in all their activities and interactions. We must have a strong desire and new commitment to clear up such a loss of trust. Both the one who betrayed and the one who is betrayed must take a hard, deep look at how they each created the betrayal. Self-reflection will see us through the Third Gate. It is a powerful piece of growth that, while potentially painful, can be profoundly healing. Know that if our action betrays another, we have betrayed ourselves first. The remedies of the Six Gates are used in the same way for these extraordinary transformations as they are for the apparently ordinary ones.

Photo by BJ Brown

The Third Gate:
Taking True Responsibility

To step into a true sense of responsibility is to release defensiveness and blame. Many people think that taking responsibility means to take on the fault or blame for the entire undesired scenario. This is not taking responsibility. In truth, it will exacerbate the entangled situation by adding resentment and regret. Taking true responsibility means that we accept responsibility for our own part and allow the other party to take responsibility for theirs. When we are in the murk of a conflict, that murkiness can feel like quicksand, pulling us deeper into the cycle of faultfinding, blaming, and defensiveness. Taking true responsibility can simplify and even create more ease through the conflict toward greater connection and freedom.

The practice of stepping into true responsibility requires us to pay attention to what we are creating.

Listen to what you choose to say about the real feelings you are experiencing. Is our response to the situation really about expressing the truth of our actions and feelings? Or are we attempting to convince the other person that their behavior is causing us to react in a certain way? True responsibility is aiming for the former. If we are feeling a sense of what is true, aware of the unarguable feelings in our heart and body, grounded in ourselves, then we are expanding our ability to respond to the other person free from blame and defense. When we are caught in the tangle of explaining, convincing, reacting, repeating what the other person is doing or should have been doing, then we are not communicating our unarguable truth. Blaming others or insisting on being right inhibits our heart from feeling what's true. Thus, we hinder our own ability to respond in a healthy way.

Another entangling dynamic is when we take on more responsibility than what truly belongs to us. I've heard many people I counsel say things like this: "I blame myself for the whole thing," or "I just take care of all of it so I can avoid the confrontation." Rather than diffusing the confrontation, this approach will ultimately inflame it because the true feelings of anger or resentment remain unspoken or even unrecognized.

Conflicts that emerge in relationships create the opportunity for healing and resolution. Ideally, we regard our relationship conflicts as a chance to discover what is underneath them—what wants to be healed. When they reemerge in a patterned way, it is a signal for us to look at what is truly our responsibility in repeating the cycle. We can create a profound shift when we recognize what we are bringing to the dynamic and step into our true sense of responsibility. Then we are more likely to shake loose the pattern's hold on our relationship.

Photo by BJ Brown

The Fourth Gate:

Facing Regrets and

Resentments

Looking squarely at our own feelings of regret and resentment is a key to unleashing our creative energy. This courageous step will broaden our capacity for more authentic and sweeter connection in our lives. It's important to identify the quality of thought, feeling, and sensation we carry around in our mind, body, and heart that are associated with regret and resentment. These particular experiential states have their own flavor and texture. Regret, for example, is likely to have a quality of sorrow or fear in it, different from, say, a fear of flying or sadness over a friend's illness. Resentment will feel different in the body than regret. Resentment is a version of anger but feels different from the anger you feel when your car door got scratched or you dropped your books in a puddle. In whatever way these feelings of regret and resentment show up, they restrict a free flow of energy that can be better used for creative expression and creating the life we really want.

Once we have identified these feelings and sensations, we then look within for what we have not yet accepted about the regret or resentment. When we lack acceptance for a situation, we become stuck in resentment and regret, which can fester into bitterness. This is where the gateway of True Responsibility may be bridged with this Facing gateway. Ask yourself what you want to be different now. What do you want to choose now? You more than likely had choices throughout the event about which you hold resentment or regret. Even if you feel you had no choice then, you have choices now about how you want to move forward. Coming into a place of acceptance and clear choosing in the present is a full step through this gateway.

*Feelings of resentment and regret
will be melted by the fire of our presence
in the moment.*

ॐ

BJ Brown

Photo by BJ Brown

The Fifth Gate:

Tending Remorse

Notice if you are feeling guilt or are telling yourself you actually are guilty. Let me clear this up for you right now: Guilt is not a feeling; guilt is a self-imposed state of mind, one that we tend to believe is imposed on us by someone else. It is the undercurrent, more than likely a feeling of fear, that most wants our attention. Guilt is based in fear. I invite you to look into it yourself. Let your heart and body be your own laboratory.

Remorse, however, comes from a genuine sense of sorrow we feel about something we may have said or done to cause pain for another person. Remorse is based in love. The experience and sensation of remorse is felt in the heart. It is a service the heart offers us in our emotional experience. Our body sensations and feelings are of great service to us if we listen deeply to the information they offer from within.

The ability to tend the remorse we feel comes from our willingness to clarify and move through the state and perception of guilt. This requires us to look truthfully at the event and those actions about which we may still carry guilt. In my experience, and from what I've heard from so many others, guilt has no flow in it. It creates stickiness, stagnation. Tuning into the truth and depth of your feelings while listening to your body-voice provides more information to you about where there is movement in your emotions and sensations. Turn to your heart about this incomplete state of guilt. The heart transforms guilt into remorse. Remorse is truly about an experience of sorrow for the action you participated in that needs closure. Tending to your feelings of sadness or sorrow, the remorse for how you have behaved in the past, will allow you to genuinely take responsibility for your actions, as in the Third Gate of Taking True Responsibility, and communicate about them in a way that can clean the slate. When you reach this point, you will find a greater sense of completion and another opening for what can begin anew.

Photo provided by iStockphoto

The Sixth Gate:

Forgiving

While it's a common lesson to "forgive and forget," I'm not convinced that one can go the distance on the forgetting. I have another take on this. The meaning of forget here is more about the freedom one feels when the experience of having forgiven is genuinely achieved. It is not to say that the incident is banished from one's conscious awareness. It is, however, being free of emotional, mental, or physical charge about it. Then that's it: the charge and attachment is what is forgotten when we truly forgive.

This is a splendid and even sublime aim. I know this to be accurate from having reached a true state of forgiveness for certain events in my life and for particular people, including myself. Yet it is not a goal we can reach prematurely. Fully identifying and freeing up our emotional expression is a primary ingredient to attaining the clarity of forgiveness.

Many people will try to feel compassion and forgiveness too close to the event that hurt them and without any time or space to feel their feelings. We need time to make a transition or perhaps to come to an ending. If there is some breach of integrity that affects the relationship—whether it's an argument, a broken agreement, an infidelity, a lie— an innate shift occurs in the relationship causing a crossroads in the couple's journey. Each person will have feelings about the nature of the transition itself that will need to be honored and tended, and their feelings resulting from the breach of trust will need attention.

This is a process, a walk around and back and forth through layers of feelings. Of all the gateways it is primarily this one that calls for the most time and patience. The other gateways are necessary to deliver us to this particular threshold of Forgiveness.

Reaching too quickly for forgiveness keeps us from thoroughly exploring our feelings. We must express these feelings. If we don't, our bodies will manifest all sorts of symptoms to get us to look more closely at what feelings we have not addressed. Sometimes we'll create another scenario, similar to the last (and the one before that and the one before that) with the same person, or someone else, to get us to feel through those emotions we previously denied. Thus, an attempt to forgive prematurely will create a toxic situation. The unfelt, squelched emotion eventually rots beneath the false gesture of forgiveness. If you still feel a charge or a flow of adrenaline at the memory of some hurtful event you thought you were "over," then you've not yet reached an authentic state of forgiveness. First allow the full acknowledgment and flow of feelings regarding the difficult event or situation. Then the path is clear for you to feel compassion and then forgiveness.

Lead with your heart. If you start out with an intention to be compassionate, kind, and forgiving, that's wonderful. It is a disservice, though, if it means you deny yourself that kindness and compassion. Give permission to yourself not to be ready to forgive someone while simultaneously holding the intention that you will.

Then see your journey all the way through, attending to your feelings and listening for your responsibility.

Beginning

The journey from a beginning of something to its end is constantly happening. So it is true that coming to the end of something brings us to a new threshold, also constantly occurring. It boggles the mind to imagine every twist and turn, every end and beginning that we each pass through in an ordinary day. Be open to the possibility of taking nothing for granted and having a grateful awareness of all the transitions in a day and in a life, great and small. To begin anew each day with the intention to be keenly aware of the transition points freshens and deepens our consciousness.

The Beginning

 و

A blank page awaits my hand.
What am I starting, here and now?
I begin a new chapter.
I begin the last chapter.
I near the end of this book -
other deaths hang in the mists.
Always at the edge, the opening, the portal.
Only a breath from beginning, and end.
Love this here.
Love the next chapter.
Love the edge, the portal, the breath.
Love the page, your hand, the end.
Love the altar of mystery.
Love this now.

 و

BJ Brown

When we find ourselves in certain transitions that feel gnarly or messy, it serves to retrace our steps back to the point where we felt most present. Look at what unfolded right after that moment of presence and awareness. Was there an interaction or transition that was difficult? Were we shaken by it or thrown off center? Was it simply that the communication was incomplete? Go back and clear up that juncture with greater awareness, using the gateways and exercises in these pages.

Turning our attention on the little transitions throughout our day is great practice for refining our ability to face the more difficult changes to come. As a reminder, here are some ordinary transitions that happen nearly every day: departing from somewhere or arriving, leaving home to go to work, leaving work to go home, leaving the office for lunch, returning to the office, ending a conversation, changing from one classroom to the next, from one meeting to the next, getting your child to school, preparing for your day, showering off your day, and heading for bed at night.

There are countless other shifts layered through all of these, creating a multifaceted dance of changes that make up the kaleidoscope of our lives.

As you look over any of these scenarios or other ordinary transitions, wonder: Did you say what you needed to say on your way out? Toss an "I love you," maybe? Were you in a sense of presence and awareness enough that these ordinary turns of the morning feel complete to you? Perhaps you were gruff with a family member or you missed a look in their eyes as you dashed out the door? Did you forget to nourish yourself? Did you leave something at home you needed for the meeting later? There really is no wrong answer. If you had a good exchange with your family, felt present for what was most important, you might have a laugh or even feel carefree that you left that item you thought you needed for the meeting. Dropping into the moment, into a state of presence while holding intention toward the sense of completion, urges us to cherish what is most important. Even when we feel sadness or challenge, the intention to live in completion can infuse these times with sweetness.

Extraordinary Is Ordinary

These are the ordinary moments in our lives. Imagine looking at them with your heart wide open. Imagine that this could be the last morning you'd ever glance back to say I love you or appreciate someone or deliver a pat on the back or a kiss on the cheek. We never know. There is no way to know if you'll see the ones you love again. We cannot know for certain when the next loss will come, or if we'll pray with our community again, or pat the dog, or tend the home, or see the flowers in our garden, hear her laugh, wipe his tears—ever again. When we recognize the reality of this persistent unknown, not theoretically nor with the logical mind—then perhaps we'll begin to accept impermanence and see how utterly extraordinary it is to be alive for these exquisite, ordinary moments. Pause to breathe with conscious awareness, even for a second, as you move through these ordinary events and allow yourself to feel the extraordinary within them. In so doing, you are growing into one who truly cherishes and appreciates the abundance in your life. Taking something or someone for granted is no longer an option. We don't have to miss anything.

The sweet moments of synchronicity, those experiences that surprise us as serendipitous, tend to be viewed as extraordinary. Being lit by the light of the moment, being present without attachment or expectation for what should happen next, will bring an awareness that these moments are happening all around us, all the time. These lucky strikes will be less a surprise and more a recognized ordinary occurrence with the extraordinary at its core.

Ordinary Is Extraordinary

As I have had the privilege of being at the bedside of several people in their dying process, witnessed them as they clearly connected the thinning veil between here and not-here, I am convinced that what we perceive as extraordinary is always with us—dressed in the ordinary.

---

*And if you could, you think you would trade it all, all the pain and suffering.
Ah—but then you'd miss the beauty of the light upon this earth,
and the sweetness of the leaving.*

ॐ

*Jane Siberry
from her song, "Calling All Angels"*

"The light upon this earth," with its changing hues, its opalescence and inspiration, is available to us every day. We witness the light upon this earth not only by gazing across the sky but also by hearing a child's laughter, or looking into a mother's eyes or feeling our lover's kiss. We witness the light in a healer's hand and in the flowers we tend in the garden. Beauty is everywhere, even in the dark, even in loss. These heart-quickening moments, the ones that feel life-altering and extraordinary, can be embraced and taken in, soul and body, in any ordinary moment. Gaze upon a sunset or place your bare feet on the earth as you walk. This is the connection between the physical and spiritual self.

The deaths and births I have witnessed are the most extraordinary experiences I have known. These are the most alluring portals, the most ineffable, the kind that reverberate down to the marrow and soul. Death and birth take place every day, on any ordinary day, and in every fleeting moment. When I welcomed those beings into the world, and when I said goodbye to those dear ones, it took not much longer than the intake and release of my own breath. Those people were here one minute, breathing life into the bone and flesh that made me, raised me, taught me, fed me, befriended me—and then in the next minute what had been filled with life was merely a shell.

To be present for the death of a loved one can be both devastating and beautiful—exquisite agony. The same journey that can be messy, painful, complex, and wrought with challenge, can simultaneously be seen and felt as sublime and infused with grace and dignity. To be present with a loved one at the ordinary moments of their last breaths is an extraordinary gift to yourself and to your loved one. It is a gift, a privilege, an initiation to see someone through this ultimate passage.

Our whole world and all the rest of our days are changed because a new baby comes into being, inhabiting his or her place. It is as though a new constellation is born. Our lives are forever changed from the moment that being comes into form here in our world. We needn't focus on the scientific intricacies of human development to see that some compelling force—an ordinary, unfathomable, quantum, and natural force beyond us—is also within us as we bloom into life and follow our season into death.

Birth and death are transformative events. The being that grows in the dark womb emerges as the infant in the mother's arms; eventually another dramatic shift occurs at the end of life when the spirit that inhabits the body leaves the shell of what was. Transformation occurs literally and metaphorically. Those who can be present to bear witness to these ultimate changes are also transformed.

The common and the amazing reside and flow within each other. We do not have to be a great American poet or a Sufi mystic to look on life with fresh eyes and hearts wide open for discovery. We are all the same, in this and so many ways: we are born into this life and we leave it when it is our time. These are the most profound—and most common—primary experiences we will ever go through. We all share this.

Between beginning and end, how we face, witness, and take responsibility for words and deeds throughout our life determines the richness and the sweetness of our leaving.

Love This Now

As I type these last pages, I sit in my living room with my first cup of coffee, my laptop computer on my lap. A small plane flies overhead, as though in slow motion, the sound of the engine lingering. Early morning light is cast over my garden, shadow dances on the aspen leaves. My beloved sits at the table on the back deck reading the New York Times. The breeze sings through the trees. I am breathing deeply, pausing to notice the intricacies of the opening day. There is a sweetness in it, a simplicity. It is ordinary. I do not know from this moment when I pause in this writing whether I'll be here at the end of this particular day. So I savor these few moments. I have a rich and abiding faith that I am meant to witness these colors, this light, those sounds, the barking dog in the distance, the chickadee out back, the faint ticking of the dining room clock, my beloved turning a page. These would still occur if I were not paying any attention. Why not pay attention? In doing so, I recognize the sacred.

Begin something and recognize the sacred in that beginning. Every human has an innate longing for connection. The natural and amazing simplicity of that longing tends to go underground. Cultural, social, religious, familial beliefs and patterns can drive this Sacred Longing into the shadows of who we really are, and when that happens, we become confused about what we truly want. Sacred Longing then turns into many other yearnings, needs, entitlements, addictions, and unhealthy relationships. We lose touch with what we really want and how we want to live and love. Recognizing we've lost touch with what is sacred is not the end. It is an opening to transformation. Becoming aware of the deeper desire, remembering the Sacred Longing, creates a new beginning. As we become more capacious for loving or appreciating what *is* now, then a beginning always awaits our attention.

Appreciation for completing and beginning comes from the same well. When we are open to discovery, willing to live complete and welcoming change, then even in the darkest moments we'll see there is something to love and appreciate. Many who have gone through extreme situations, felt tragic loss, experienced natural disaster or trauma, been through life threatening addiction, or near death experiences have come through them with the understanding that some great lesson or blessing graced them. Such events can be the impetus for accessing the ability to love what is and to appreciate living complete and beginning anew.

Looking in on your internal landscape and making the conscious choice to journey through *The Six Gates of Completion* tap the well of love and appreciation for *what is* right now. The journey will free the flow of energy and aliveness and will be stable ground for your integrity. The journey begins now, on this sublime and ordinary day.

Love this now. Begin it now.

෨   ෨   ෨

PART III:
SOUL PLAY

෨   ෨   ෨

ॐ ॐ ॐ

The Soul Play exercises may be explored using the
available space below or by using your own journal.
Let this be a private, sacred place for you to go inward
and respond to these exercises. This is your personal
experiment. Give yourself permission to explore in
your own time, at your own pace, playing with as
many or as few of these suggestions as is comfortable
for you. Notice if you feel an aversion to any particular
exercise. Those are more likely to be the profound and
revelatory ones for you to explore.

1. Increase Awareness of Daily Transitions

Play this week with catching yourself in the transitions and shifts in your day. Let's plant the seed now as you read and try this on: Tomorrow as you kiss your kids or honey goodbye, set off for work, get to this meeting or end that phone call—whatever transition you choose—take notice of what is happening in your body.

What do you notice about your experience?

_____

_____

_____

_____

_____

_____

_____

_____

_____

_____

Describe how you are doing, reacting, responding through these turns in the day.

_____

_____

_____

_____

_____

_____

_____

_____

_____

_____

_____

_____

_____

_____

_____

_____

_____

What do you notice about your breathing?

_____

_____

_____

_____

_____

_____

_____

_____

Did you forget to tell someone something?

_____

_____

_____

_____

_____

_____

_____

_____

Are you feeling sad or irritated and aren't sure why?

_____

_____

_____

_____

_____

_____

_____

_____

Did you withhold something in some conversation?

_____

_____

_____

_____

_____

_____

_____

_____

Make a list of changes in your day.

_____

_____

_____

_____

_____

_____

_____

_____

How would you like to come through these changes more smoothly?

_____

_____

_____

_____

_____

_____

Are you creating enough space and time in your life to express fully what needs to be expressed? Answer yes, no, or sometimes:

If you answered no to certain things on your list, those are the areas that await your creative exploration. The next steps will serve that very thing.

Please note that if your list encompasses the larger life-transforming kinds of events, stay the course. I'll be addressing those more deeply in exercises to come.

Highlight those shifts in the day when you felt satisfied. You came through a shift smoothly, spoke the truth, or completed a project. Give yourself some loving appreciation for doing so. To take notice of these healthy moves through transitions is a fine way to expand your capacity to continue to do them well. Tell yourself, "Yes, well done!"

2. Set Your Intentions

Take a few minutes each morning to write down three intentions for how you want to create your day. State more than three intentions if you like. If you have not practiced this before, I encourage you to start with three and work your way up. It's best to express in affirmative terms, discerning what it is you want, what you want to do, how you intend to respond in certain situations, rather than expressing what you don't want. For example, "I intend to speak honestly with so-and-so and to listen to what she has to say to me," instead of "I intend to not get into an argument with so-and-so." Instead of "My intention for today is to stop getting down on myself when I'm running late," try this: "My intention today is to plan better and to be on time. I also intend to take a gentler look at myself and what I'm creating in my day." You get the idea.

You may want to keep a journal for daily intentions. Meanwhile you can try it here.

_____
_____
_____
_____
_____
_____
_____
_____
_____
_____
_____
_____
_____
_____
_____
_____
_____
_____

3. Review Your Day

Tune in with yourself at the end of your day and take a look at your journal. Look at the intentions you wrote that morning. Glance over the events of your day while noticing your energy, body sensation, feelings you may have as you view your day. Were you able to follow through with your intentions—that is, did you keep the agreements you made that morning? Let yourself feel some appreciation toward yourself and for anyone who might have aided you in following through with your intentions. Notice what comes up for you if you did not come to the end of your day fulfilling your intention. Jot down a few words in your journal about this. Let the process teach you to refine how you state your intentions. Let me reiterate: It is OK if you discover what you want by first seeing what you don't want. Then, as you write down your intentions, reframe your statement so that it affirmatively expresses what you do want by setting the intention.

Now try it here:

_____

_____

_____

_____

_____

_____

_____

_____

_____

_____

_____

_____

_____

_____

_____

_____

_____

_____

4. List Your Incompletions

Ask yourself in what area you are feeling at loose ends in the four primary incompletions:

- ∽ Promises unkept.
- ∽ Actions you feel guilty about.
- ∽ Important unspoken communications.
- ∽ Significant resentments or regrets.

Is there anyone with whom you feel incomplete?

_____

_____

What resentments or regrets do you still carry?

_____

_____

_____

_____

_____

_____

_____

Notice how and where in your body you may be holding —or contracting around—such resentments or regrets.

_____

_____

_____

_____

_____

Is there some action you continue to feel guilty or remorseful about?

_____

_____

_____

_____

_____

_____

_____

_____

_____

What promises have you made that are still left hanging?

_____

_____

_____

_____

_____

_____

_____

_____

_____

_____

If big feelings come up about any of this, move your body. Go for a walk. Turn some music on and dance around your living room. Making noise, vocalizing—even animal sounds and gibberish—bouncing up and down, and jiggling are ways to shake up any excess energy that is caught in your body and needs to be released.

5. Make a Mask of Incompletion

To creatively express the many faces of completion, create a collage of the mask/face. Pick a persona or façade you use to avoid completing something. For example, you may have an inner rebel who resists changes that would allow you to soften and feel resolved. Create a collage of this rebel and of the sort of dust the rebel kicks up to veil completion. Mask-making is another playful and profound option to put into physical form whatever psychically or emotionally blocks your way. You may choose to do this artful expression on the expansive forward moving energy in you as well.

The face of forgiveness—what would that collage look like? And the face of reconciliation, or birth, or the heart bursting open—what would these look like in your physical expression? I invite you to step into the creative flow that is organically your own.

6. Move Your Body Through Incompletion

Play out the masks, act them out. Put on some music and move that energy through your body in freestyle movement or dance. Movement is powerful for shaking loose any energy you might be stuck in. Try on the façade or mask and allow yourself to embody it. Exaggerate its quality or its message by playing it out, acting the part to the hilt. When you can move and shake or dance your body in this way— with the intention of shaking loose the grip of your impostor—you'll find it frees you up and more authenticity can rise to the foreground.

If your style or your mask of incompletion is really about not moving (resistance), you can still play that out. Simply feel what it's like to exaggerate the stuck feeling. For example, you might curl up tightly and contract your muscles, curl in more, hold your breath —more—more—then—RELEASE! Try that on.

What do you notice? Take note of the sensations you feel when you release the contraction.

_____

_____

_____

_____

_____

_____

_____

_____

_____

_____

_____

_____

Now shake it off. This will help to loosen the grip of that particular holding pattern or facade.

Identifying the areas in which you are incomplete is the first big step.

Your movement can also be slower paced, or quiet, as in a walking meditation. The key is to move with awareness and mindfulness.

7.   Write a Letter You Won't Send

Letter writing, with robust intention, is a powerful way to move your thoughts and feelings to deeper layers of clarity and resolve. Start by writing letters you won't send. For example, if you are sorting through big feelings about someone, write what I call the "let 'em have it" letter. Spew and vent and even point fingers. As you do this, notice what happens in your body. Breathe your way through the sensations. If your intention is to clear up loose ends, this letter will naturally send you to the next layer. You are closer to completion as you peel through these layers.

_____

_____

_____

_____

_____

_____

_____

_____

_____

_____

_____

_____

_____

_____

_____

_____

_____

_____

_____

_____

_____

_____

_____

_____

_____

_____

_____

8. Express What Is True

Write a letter that expresses the truth of your feelings, the truth that you came to by checking in with your body.

Write about how you created this incompletion and express the responsibility you intend to take to resolve the situation and move forward.

_____

_____

_____

_____

_____

_____

_____

_____

_____

_____

_____

You may want to write another letter as you move through the layers of your thoughts and feelings about the person and the situation. Eventually you may even want to express your feelings in person.

Keeping a journal is a way to make sacred and private space for your expression. You might want to write the letters in the journal. Your journal is a powerful vessel where you can write the early-stage letters and release the sting of stuck feelings. Another profound release is to burn the letters in a safe way and safe place, like a wood-burning fireplace. You could shred them and use the paper in your compost or use it as mulch. These are fine metaphors for transmuting the negativity you once held.

9. Wonder about Closure

Make a list of the people you'd like to have closure with and situations you'd like to change so you can create an opening for something new. Each of these gateways instructs you about how to find your own loose ends. One profound way to approach this is to wonder about this question (fill in the name of the person):

If _____ had three months to live, how would I feel?

_____

_____

_____

_____

_____

_____

_____

_____

What would I want to say to him or her?

_____

_____

_____

_____

_____

_____

_____

Would I want to go to his or her side? And if so, what might keep me from following that desire?

_____

_____

_____

_____

_____

_____

_____

_____

This is about your own personal integrity now. Possibly some of you who are reading this might think, "Good riddance." But the burden of what was incomplete between you continues to sit with you. Go deeper. What do you need to do or say that is a responsible action toward your own freedom?

Similarly, wonder about what it would feel like to be told that you had only three months to live.

What incompletion is still dangling for you?

_____

_____

_____

_____

_____

_____

_____

_____

_____

_____

Ask yourself to whom you would want to express your
love, your appreciation, your remorse, your truth.

_____

_____

_____

_____

_____

_____

_____

_____

10. Explore Layers of Feeling

Consider each gate individually, or view them in any combination. However you proceed, think of someone or something with whom or about which you'd like to create a sense of completion. As you pan over this in your mind and heart, start the layers of letter writing. If there is still emotional charge that feels venomous to you when you think of this person or situation, you are still at the layer of defense and blame, maybe even rage. You are bound to create a great clearing for yourself as you write through these emotional layers, even though it may seem a daunting exercise at first. Hold the desire for completion in your vision. The first letter in this case would be the "let 'em have it" letter. This is only an exercise. You won't send this letter. It is merely a place for you to pour and spew those stories that still hold a negative charge. Let yourself bark!

As you move through this layer with a willingness to discover your truth, you'll become ready for the next layer. Read through the first letter. Search for the essence of your feeling, such as "I feel sad, mad, scared . . . ." Or "When you lied to me, my heart hurt for weeks. I felt a spasm in my neck I feared would never end." In this letter, you are going for the truth of what your physical and emotional body is experiencing.

In the next layer, you are writing about your responsibility. For example, you might discover a recurring pattern you are involved in. This could sound like, "I see that I have allowed this to take place in other situations in my life. I've tended not to trust my intuition in the past. I've become aware that if I continue not to be honest with myself, then someone or something is bound to mirror that back to me. I feel sad about this and intend to listen to myself and be more honest about how I'm feeling."

Eventually, you might want to create a letter at this deeper level of expression, a letter that you send. You might even create such clarity for yourself that you extend an invitation to the other person to create completion together. When you find yourself with such an opportunity, you have a chance to use the Six Gates of Completion as your guides and allies to communicate directly.

If the person is dead, lost, or unwilling to participate, I encourage you to go through this process anyway. I've found it incredibly momentous for myself and my students to engage in this process. Ask a friend or counselor to hear your letter. It is up to you what feedback you would most like to receive from them. For this, however, I'm suggesting only open and compassionate witnesses. Words back from your witness are not really necessary, only their presence. Once you've read and expressed yourself, you might burn the letters or shred them and use them for mulch. Another creative use is to crumple them up or tear them and use them in a collage. These are ceremonial ways to create the next thing, to open the window, opening yourself to a new beginning.

11. Meditate

Take from 15 to 30 minutes for some quiet, private space. Music is a profound vehicle to take you into a deeper, more relaxed state of being, or you may want to do this in silence. If you choose music, play something instrumental, no lyrics. (Please see the Resource Yourself section for contemplative music recommendations.)

Find a relaxed, comfortable position. Closing your eyes, begin breathing slowly and deeply, in and out through your nose. As you settle in, be mindful of each of these Six Gates of Completion. Imagine you are moving along a path, somewhere that is soothing to your soul. It could be a lovely place that is familiar to you. It might be fresh, new territory. Notice whatever inner landscape you see in your mind's eye. Breathe slowly and deeply down into your soft belly. Now imagine you've stepped into a circle. It may be in a natural setting—a circle of trees or stones—or perhaps it is a chamber. You feel a quickening of energy or inspiration as you see that this place holds great possibilities for you, even though they may be a mystery to you now.

Imagine that you are surrounded by six gateways. Turn around gently in a circle and listen to your heart and intuition for which gateway you are to cross first.

As you see yourself encircled by the gates, ask yourself in what areas you feel incomplete. Notice what gate calls to you.

Or do you feel pulled? You choose. Gently visualize yourself moving through these gateways, listening internally for what most wants your loving attention.

Notice as you breathe.

Give yourself permission to walk this contemplative pathway to and from the different Gates of Completion. When you feel complete for the moment with your journey, write about your experience.

What did you see?

_____

_____

_____

_____

_____

_____

_____

_____

What came up in your awareness, your heart, and your body?

_____

_____

_____

_____

_____

_____

_____

Was anyone there to greet you?

_____

_____

_____

_____

_____

_____

What did they say or ask of you?

_____

_____

_____

_____

_____

_____

_____

_____

_____

_____

Remember, you can revisit this inner space as much as you like. After doing the meditation, you may find more information, thoughts, feelings pop up for you randomly. Trust that you've invited your inner teacher to be more present with you. Listen to your dreams. Write about your experiences. Take at least five minutes in the middle of your day for solitude and pause. While in that space, ask yourself what is happening in your body. This is something you can do many times—even hundreds of times—throughout your entire day. If this comes easily to you, stay tuned in with yourself and your body's voice as much as is comfortable for you. If this is new to you, try it this way: Listen for any sensations from within. You are listening to your senses. For example, notice if there is something you can smell in the air. Can you hear a bird outside? Are you aware of rumblings in your tummy? Could it be hunger, or digestion, or perhaps fear? Are you feeling any aches or pains? Simply notice whatever you notice. You could say to yourself or aloud what is coming up for you. Writing it down is also an option. However, it is likely that your senses will give you information far more quickly than your hand can take note of them.

This is a fine sensory awareness exercise I teach to my clients, and they often find it is quite deepening and meditative. I encourage you to keep your eyes closed while you are checking in to listen and feel. With practice, you will heighten your sensory acuity. Here's mine right now:

Deep breath with my eyes closed. Feeling the keys under my finger tips. My typing is slowing down. My breath gets tight in my solar plexus. I open my eyes, look at the screen. Breath flows more easily. My right eye has an itch. My toes feel cozy in my new socks, warm. Deep breath. I'm feeling a clenching pinch in my right shoulder, front side. I close my eyes. I feel a tickle in my nose. Breathing. Judging the pace of my typing. Thinking. Eyes open—stop to rub my right eye. I see the sunlight coming in the window to my left. I feel a pleasant flow, delight in my chest. I can still taste the coffee in my mouth. My calves are chilly—and so on.

When you take even a few minutes to deeply tune in, you exercise your sensory awareness, increasing your capacity to trust your own senses and intuition. It is as though you are stretching, strengthening another muscle you didn't know you had. Just as in meditation, if your mind starts to go off in a story and you find yourself thinking, then simply say to yourself, thinking. Then come back to your breath and notice what you are feeling or sensing. Allow yourself to stay with your sensations and feel the meditative qualities of this exercise. The more you play with this, letting your thinking mind relax for a little while, the more fun you will have fine-tuning the ability to hear your inner voice and your body.

Go to the next level by tuning into your emotional body. You can use what you've already practiced, listening to your body voice, borrowing from the list of feelings and sensations. While doing this, ask yourself for the deeper awareness of what is happening emotionally.

Are you feeling sad, mad, happy, scared, or sexual feelings?

_____

_____

Your physical and emotional bodies are stretching to meet one another; they are one. They give you deeper self-awareness and alignment as you grow more available to really tuning in to yourself.

This exercise can be very grounding. Sometimes I use this if I'm having trouble sleeping. The intention and focus of tuning in so deeply allows your brain and body to relax into the moment. This practice allows your truest emotions to have more space and clarity.

12. Create a Collage

In your next several journal entries, create a collage portraying the predominant feeling you are experiencing that day. Choose your regular journal or a larger tablet, canvas, poster board, sketch pad— whatever works best for your creative expression at that particular time. The collage provides an expansive, right-brained presentation of what is percolating for you in the emotional realm. The medium of collage allows us to choose imagery and color to convey what we often inadequately attempt with words. For example, you might feel a lightness of being one morning, happy, carefree, rested. The images that stand out while you page through a magazine for this exercise would be softer, brighter, than say if you woke up feeling anxious or angry. If I woke happy and well-rested, I might select images with sunlight, white sand beach, someone meditating, or a couple holding hands. If I woke feeling irritated or not well-rested, the images I select might be more fiery, like a picture of a lightning storm.

13. Journal about Incompletion

Create a quiet space where you will not have any interruptions. Give yourself at least 15 minutes. Allow yourself to really relax into this time and space for you. Write down a few examples of situations in which you are feeling incomplete. No need to do much processing right now. Later you can take time to explore what feels incomplete.

For now, just allow awareness to come to the surface and name the incompletion clearly for yourself. These can be what you identify as big or small incompletions.

_____

_____

_____

_____

_____

_____

_____

_____

Pace yourself. If you want to start with one that is a little deal rather than a big deal, that's just fine.

Here's an example:

I was at the big staff meeting last week. I saw John look across the room with what I thought was an angry glare. I felt scared. I've chosen not to interact with him the rest of the week. My belly feels jumpy and I lose my breath when I see him at work.

OK? That's the first step. In this case the truth is that you feel scared, your belly feels jumpy, you're not breathing fully when these feelings come up, and you are choosing to avoid John. Good start. So—the next question is simple, yet powerful: How would you like this to be different? What do you want? Let the words flow through the pen in a stream of consciousness. If we use childlike wisdom, we might say "I don't want my stomach to feel jumpy when I see John." Or "I don't like turning away from him when I see him there, I don't want to feel scared to talk to him."

Now what do you want? Simply notice what you notice and jot it down.

_____

_____

_____

_____

_____

_____

_____

_____

_____

_____

_____

_____

Notice what happens in your body as you become clearer about what you really want. Here is an answer that is out of your control: "I don't want John to glare at me." Let yourself respond by focusing on how you feel and how you can take responsibility for your own well-being.

14. Collage Your Entanglements

You can do this on a couple of pages in your journal or you can use poster board, foam board, a box. Collage is one of the easiest art forms, especially for those who may not see themselves as artistic or creative. Let yourself be free of judgment, and keep your collage as simple or as profound as you are moved in the moment. Anything goes here. Collage can take any shape, size, or form and can be created with all sorts of materials.

Gather magazines and scissors—or just tear out pages. Use old letters or notes or photos, glue sticks, and whatever type of canvas you prefer. Name it "Collage of Entanglements." As you are paging through pictures and words in the magazines, hold the intention that you are exposing this entanglement. This creation becomes a symbol of the entanglement in physical form. Feelings will arise. Let them flow through you and they will contribute to the authenticity and spontaneity of your creative expression.

15. Collage Your Liberation

You may want to explore another layer of expression after your entanglements feel fully revealed. Your honest and conscious look at your entanglements is a step toward cutting through your attachment to them. The next collage could be created with this question in mind: What does this entanglement look like unsnarled, unbound, cleared up, complete? Create a collage on the feeling of being liberated.

16. Journal about Transition

Describe the nature of your chrysalis.

_____

_____

_____

_____

_____

_____

_____

What are you between right now, if anything?

_____

_____

_____

_____

_____

_____

_____

_____

Is there a time in your life when you have felt yourself in a void or a mystery? Describe that experience.

_____

_____

_____

_____

_____

_____

_____

_____

_____

_____

_____

_____

_____

_____

_____

_____

_____

_____

17.   Dance the Transition

Allow your body to move and express your "transition dance." I'm not suggesting you dance the limbo, though you might be tempted. Here's the idea: Imagine yourself flying on a trapeze, swinging gracefully back and forth on one bar. See the other bar headed your way as an invitation, calling you to it. Imagine yourself taking the leap. Dance that and notice what comes up, what you are feeling, body sensations. I invite you to move your body without judging your movements. If you like, pop in a CD. I recommend movie sound tracks or instrumental music so that only the music evokes your feelings and impulses to move, rather than lyrics you might use to tell yourself a story.

18. Explore the Tarot

If you don't already have a Tarot deck, go to your local bookstore and try out samples of Tarot decks to find one that especially speaks to you. If there are new age sorts of shops in your area, you may get more detailed information about the types of decks available.

A few of my particular favorite decks are The Voyager Tarot, The Atavist Deck, Osho Zen Tarot, Mother Peace Tarot. There are also decks called Soul Cards. These are not based on traditional Tarot. There are no words on the cards, yet the images are so profound and evocative that simply gazing on an image can stir your inner teacher to give you just the information you seek. The same is also true of the more traditional Tarot decks. If you are in a particular transition that is bringing up some unanswered questions, you can turn a card or do a reading for yourself.

I invite you to sometimes play with only the images and pictures, ignoring the words. This will help you use the more creative, right side of your brain and rely less on personality or ego. Sometimes too many words and placing meaning on them is the very thing that keeps an answer out of reach.

19. Collage Your Crossroads

Remember, your collage can be created through very mixed media. It needn't be flat, unless that's what feels right to you. For example, using small boxes, beads, different textured yarns or ribbons add depth and flow to a collage. A shoe box or cigar box makes a wonderful template to create collage. Decorating inside and out, front and back, can highlight metaphors like past-present, external-internal.

Think of the current crossroads you face, the nature of it, its terrain, your feelings and sensations. Is it chaotic or flowing? Is it still or stuck? It may be dazzling or dreary. As you wonder and feel into the nature of your current life crossroads, flip through magazines and journal entries. My suggestion is to not spend too much time going through the pictures and images. Give yourself about an hour, maybe two at the most, to go through these items. Then create. Let your process be organic. The objects you choose will make their way onto the collage in just their right place.

20. Journal Your Grief

Take some gentle time and space to wonder on what or whom you are grieving today. Is there something or someone in particular that resides in a deep place of grief for you right now? Stay in the simplicity of what is true. It could sound like this, for instance: "Today is Wednesday and I'm thinking of my friend who died ten years ago. I feel sad. I feel love for her and warmth in my chest. We laughed so much together. I'm smiling now. We were close to each other. I didn't get to say goodbye before she died." And so on. Use the simplest truest statements about your experience and what you are sensing now about it. Even in the truth telling, there is room for celebration.

Try it now:

_____

_____

_____

_____

_____

_____

_____

_____

_____

_____

_____

_____

_____

_____

_____

_____

_____

_____

_____

_____

_____

_____

_____

_____

21. Write Letters about Grief

You could write letters to assist you in your grief and move you toward celebration. For example, write a letter of appreciation to the one you grieve. Or perhaps you are grieving a group or an overall situation. Let yourself contemplate what you received or learned from them or from the experience. Thank them and say goodbye.

_____

_____

_____

_____

_____

_____

_____

_____

_____

_____

_____

22.   Collage Your Grief

Allow yourself to collage this person or your relationship to this person. Even if you have no memorabilia pertaining to them, you can flip through magazines and find images that jump out saying, "This was her" or "This was our connection."

23. Create an Altar

This can be as simple or as elaborate as you like. I suggest that the altar be placed in a small, sacred space in a private room or even a special corner of a table. You might put on the altar a candle or an old photograph, a crystal or a small bunch of wild flowers, or a poem. Choose objects that lift your heart. As you create your altar, you may experience deep feelings that evoke tears or sadness. Allow the feelings to flow through you, and ask yourself what is the source of your feelings.

Do you miss someone? Do you long for their love? Simply notice what you notice. Notice the sensation in your body. Breathe and let sound come through your throat and your mouth.

_____

_____

_____

_____

_____

The Six Gates of Completion

_____

_____

_____

_____

_____

_____

_____

_____

_____

_____

_____

_____

_____

_____

_____

_____

_____

_____

_____

_____

24. Journal about Completion

What is a current event in your life that you intend to see through?

_____

_____

_____

_____

_____

_____

_____

_____

_____

_____

_____

_____

_____

_____

_____

_____

Describe the feelings you have as you face whatever you wish to bring to completion.

_____

_____

_____

_____

_____

_____

_____

_____

_____

_____

_____

_____

_____

_____

_____

_____

_____

What in your past would you like to understand now to gain a greater sense of closure?

_____

_____

_____

_____

_____

_____

_____

_____

_____

_____

_____

_____

_____

_____

_____

_____

_____

25. Write a Eulogy

To "eulogize" is to offer good words. Write a eulogy for a situation, issue, or the person who is part of your incompletion.

_____

_____

_____

_____

_____

_____

_____

_____

_____

_____

_____

_____

_____

_____

26. Uncover What You Want

Imagine that you only have six months left to live. What would you want?

_____

_____

_____

_____

_____

_____

_____

_____

_____

_____

_____

_____

_____

_____

Who immediately comes to mind as someone with whom you wish to find completion?

_____

_____

What would you most truly want to say, and to whom?

_____

_____

_____

_____

_____

_____

_____

_____

_____

_____

_____

_____

27. Write Your Own Eulogy

What good words would you want to be spoken of you
when you die?

_____

_____

_____

_____

_____

_____

_____

_____

_____

_____

_____

_____

_____

_____

The Six Gates of Completion

_____

_____

_____

_____

_____

_____

_____

_____

_____

_____

_____

_____

_____

_____

_____

_____

_____

_____

_____

28. Write a Letter to Your Longing

Write a letter to your Longing. Look beneath the content of what you think you want—a car, a good relationship, more money—and muse on the depth of what your heart and soul really long for. You don't need to judge yourself for wanting such things. This is about going to a deeper level of self-inquiry.

_____

_____

_____

_____

_____

_____

_____

_____

_____

_____

_____

_____

The Six Gates of Completion

_____

_____

_____

_____

_____

_____

_____

_____

_____

_____

_____

_____

_____

_____

_____

_____

_____

_____

_____

_____

Ask your Longing what you must complete before you may create your soul's desire.

_____

_____

_____

_____

_____

_____

_____

_____

_____

_____

_____

_____

_____

_____

_____

_____

Ask your Longing what you must start before you can move in that direction.

_____

_____

_____

_____

_____

_____

_____

_____

_____

_____

_____

_____

_____

_____

_____

_____

29. Practice a Mantra

Practice "love this now" as a mantra. Hold the intention that when you say to yourself "love this now," you are letting the energy of love access your heart. The mantra doesn't have to bring you to some gooey, happy place. If it does, fine. For example, use the mantra in a walking meditation. You simply go for a walk and as you move, repeat internally the words "love this now." If you are comfortable saying the words aloud, try that for part of your walk. Notice what sensations and emotions come to the surface. After your walk, jot down in your journal what you noticed on your walk.

You can also practice this in situations you find less than ideal. Perhaps you are at a meeting at work and something is getting on your nerves. Try this mantra, repeating it gently to yourself, and simply notice what happens. You might say the mantra and hear another part of yourself say, "No way," or "No! I don't love this meeting," and you are in an argument with yourself. Stay with it. Now look around. Take a soft-belly breath. Look out the window at something beautiful, or notice a lovely painting on the wall. Notice the comfortable clothing you chose to wear. Keep saying the mantra. Soon you will notice that you are even more in the moment, less attached to the irritation of the meeting and more present for yourself and what is real or what holds beauty within and around you.

30. Complete and Share

Complete something, anything, today. Watch yourself keenly and with tenderness. Notice what you notice. Notice where there is ease in you. Notice that even if it was a small task, you feel a sense of satisfaction. Tell a friend about your experience.

31. Begin and Share

Begin something, anything today. Watch yourself with wonder and openness to discovery. Notice what you notice. Notice what the wanting feels like in your body. Step toward what you want. Tell a friend of your experience.

❧   ❧   ❧

RESOURCE YOURSELF

❧   ❧   ❧

৯৯   ৯৯   ৯৯

It is evolutionary—perhaps even revolutionary—to take full and active responsibility for our own health and well being. I make recommendations here for you to resource yourself both internally and externally as you continue the practice of conscious completion. I have engaged in all of these activities and modalities, and I trust their usefulness in enhancing wellness and your capacity to traverse the various kinds and vast terrain of completion. Experiment wisely, seeking recommendations or referrals from sources you trust, and continue in-depth exploration through journaling and the Soul Play exercises. Weave good, balanced doses of rest and play into your days. The more resources you have, the more easily you can create a joyful and vibrant life, even when you are facing endings or beginnings that are difficult to accept.

Here are a few of the many activities you can engage in that focus on movement and the body. These will support your well-being from the inside out, so to speak.

- ❧ Body Mantra, Boulder, CO (www.body-mantra.com)
- ❧ NIA (Neuro Integrative Action)—Founders and Directors, Debbie and Carlos Rosas, Portland, Oregon (www.NIA.com)
- ❧ Martial Arts
- ❧ Dance
- ❧ Pilates
- ❧ Swimming, especially in natural settings

Then there are healing modalities you can receive from trained, caring professionals. These resources help support you during times of transition while also contributing to general health and well-being in mind, body, and spirit.

- ❧ Massage
- ❧ Cranial-Sacral Therapy
- ❧ Acupuncture
- ❧ Ayurvedic Medicine
- ❧ Chinese Medicine
- ❧ Shamanic Healing—Foundation for Shamanic Studies, Michael Harner, Founder

- ❧ Energy work, such as Reiki and Jin Shin
- ❧ Hakomi—Hakomi Institute, Ashland, Oregon. Ron Kurtz, Founder and Director
- ❧ Body-Centered Psychotherapy or coaching
- ❧ Spiritual Counseling
- ❧ Homeopathy
- ❧ Holistic Chiropractic
- ❧ Trauma Touch Therapy™—Colorado School of Healing Arts
- ❧ Naturopathy

Consider using these gifts from nature to deepen your presence and attention more holistically.

- ❧ Hot mineral baths or hot springs.
- ❧ Bach Flower Remedies—Walnut and Rescue Remedy are useful for transitions. You can find these in your local health food stores, Vitamin Cottage, or Whole Foods.
- ❧ Young Living Essential Oils.
- ❧ Spend more time in the natural world.

These activities are worth exploring either in solitude or with others to uplift and increase a sense of presence and vitality.

- Breath work—Some of the modalities already mentioned incorporate breath work exercises. Read *Conscious Breathing* by Dr. Gay Hendricks.
- Yoga
- Meditation
- Chanting, singing, toning
- Retreats
- Intentional walking or walking meditation
- Spend a day or just a few hours in silence.
- Movies—Spiritual Cinema (www.spiritualcinema.com), Independent, and Sundance are wonderful sources for movies with a deeper message, meaning, and inspiration. See Recommended Viewing for some of my favorites.

Let your creativity flow. Here are a few examples of playing with creative expression.

- ❧ Painting or drawing.
- ❧ Writing—On your own or in a writing group.
- ❧ Conscious Collage—I offer Art of Passage Playshops, and I also design custom workshops and retreats for you, your family, company, community, or any group you'd like to involve in a soulful and creative exploration on just about any subject. Check my web site for details: www.SomaCoach.com.
- ❧ Gardening.

Explore the following to expand your compassionate heart. Bringing conscious awareness and robust intention from your heart to these activities is healing for your soul.

- ❧ Appreciation—Speak your appreciation and gratefulness for yourself, your choices, your loved ones, your work place and co-workers, nature, for being alive. Be specific as you name what you feel grateful for.

- ❧ Create more meaningful, easy time with family, animals, friends, and community.
- ❧ Give your presence and time to someone who is dying.
- ❧ Community—Whether spiritual and social, spending time in community can be deeply enriching. You could create your own Soul Play group that meets once a month to share and support your lives and the changes and completions you're experiencing, or work through the Soul Play exercises together.

It is not necessary to explore all of these resources, though that could be fun if you give yourself time, permission, and space. These are suggestions based on more than 25 years of my own exploration, some that I have integrated into my daily life. I use what is most applicable to the situation I face in the moment. Play with what rings true for you. You may already have a good portion of such resources integrated into your own days, into your own hearts. Notice if there are activities or resources I have left out that are especially appealing to you. Make your own list and begin to create action steps that bring you aliveness, peace, pleasure, and satisfaction.

Recommended Reading

Many books are available today that teach us and expand our awareness in myriad areas of life. For deepening relationship skills, I recommend *Conscious Loving* by Drs. Gay and Kathlyn Hendricks and *Undefended Love* by Jett Psaris, Ph.D., and Marlena S. Lyons, Ph.D. They offer practical tools for positive change, and they teach you how to enrich connection and commitment with yourself and others. For exploring intimate relationships from a more spiritual perspective, *Anam Chara* by John O'Donaghue, *Journey of the Heart* by John Wellwood, and *Soul Mates* by Thomas Moore are at the top of my list. While they are more grounded in the work of the soul, they also offer practical applications for creating healthy, conscious relationships.

I first became aware of Stephen and Ondrea Levine's work in the late '80's. They've done a great deal of research and work in the area of death and dying. I highly recommend *Who Dies* by Stephen

Levine, which gives us a heightened and intimate understanding of our own dying and losing those we love. The work of Elizabeth Kubler-Ross is also highly respected in the study of death and dying. I recommend her book *Life Lessons.*

Comfortable with Uncertainty, by Pema Chodron, has an orientation in Buddhist tradition and teachings. It is a wonderful exploration in facing the unknown and facing change. *Don't Bite the Hook* is another of Pema Chodron's beautiful works. This one teaches us how to directly face our anger and resentments in more conscious and responsible ways.

David Whyte is one of my favorite poets. I highly recommend that you listen to him recite his and others' poetry. He has a brilliant way of delivering a piece so that it moves right into the heart. His book of poems, *House of Belonging,* can be read repeatedly to get you through transition, loss, even existential angst. It's a beauty.

Transitions—Prayers and Declarations for a Changing Life, by Julia Cameron, is a sweet and

243

profound companion through rites of passage or ordinary everyday changes. A nice one to pick up and open randomly to any page, you're likely to find just the pearl you need.

Sacred Contracts, by Caroline Myss, takes you on a journey through the archetypes toward greater understanding of how we come together and interact in relationships. Any works of the Sufi or other mystics, such as Rumi, Mirabai, and Hafiz, will pull on your heartstrings and deepen your soul connections. Their works are great companions through our human longing and desire for the Beloved.

Recommended Listening

Soundtracks! I highly recommend listening to different film scores for deepening a visualization or meditation. Listen with intention. The music can take you into a deeper, almost lucid-dream state. Music without lyrics can evoke wonderful imagery and messages from your inner teacher. Here are a few I've used in my workshops: *Power of One*, really good if you want to move and dance. *Far From Heaven, Whale Rider, Frida*, and *The Piano* are all good for stirring the soul. Most of the songs from these soundtracks do not have lyrics, which is preferred if you're using them for imagery meditation. The soundtrack from *Once* is great for moving through relationship transitions and feelings of anger, love, and yearning.

For meditation or relaxation I recommend *December* by George Winston, *A Word In The Wind* by 2002, and *Keys to the Soul* by Matt Schanandord.

I find Eric Whitacre's choral arrangements to be among the most surprising and heart wrenching music I've ever heard. I especially love the album, *Cloudburst*.

I suggest listening to Samuel Barber's "Adagio for Strings, Op. 11" by the Smithsonian Chamber Players, and "Adagio for Strings, Op. 11" by the Choir of Trinity College, Cambridge. The "Adagio for Strings" pierces and heals the heart at the same time. I know of no other piece that can open my heart more surely than this one.

All of this music can be played while you're moving through the Soul Play Exercises. Playing this type of music while making collage will help you use more of your right brain or whole brain.

Recommended Viewing

I encourage you to view any of these films with conscious intention. This is a very different way of witnessing the process and flow of a story line than just curling up on the couch with your popcorn. As is true with music, holding an intention while watching a film can stir your inner teacher and bring up the personal things your psyche is ready to reveal to you. For example, *Antonia's Line, Cinema Paradiso, Frida, Whale Rider*, and *Long Life, Happiness and Prosperity* all address issues we face about family and intimate relationship.

Reflect on movies such as *Far From Heaven, The Piano, Brokeback Mountain* and *American Beauty* when you want to recognize your own issues about withholding, commitment, and betrayal.

Watch *The Hours* when you are wondering about what it means to be authentic, true to yourself. This film can stir so much on the subject of closure and completion.

K-Pax and *What Dreams May Come* are a mix of fantasy and reality. They both affect our ideas about how to deal with intense loss and trauma and coming to our own terms on how to contend with severe experiences.

If you want to watch movies with meaning with your children, I recommend *The Education of Little Tree, Pay It Forward, Field of Dreams,* and *Liar Liar*.

There are so many books and movies and recordings available that can inspire and support you in deepening your desire to create healthy completion and closure. All films mentioned here are great examples to teach you what completion is and is not.

About the Author

BJ Brown was raised on the north shore of Long Island, New York, where she learned some of her most profound lessons in completion and closure. She left New York for Colorado to attend undergraduate school and received her B.A. in Sociology and Criminal Justice, and later received her M.A. in Social Work with a concentration in Treatment. BJ began her private practice in Counseling in 1988. Since then her studies have expanded into more holistic and body-centered psychotherapy and spiritually oriented approaches. Her certifications include addictions counseling (CACII), Integrative Body Psychotherapy (CIBP), Trauma Touch Therapy™, Reiki Master, and Body-Mind Vibrance and Conscious Relationship Coach.

BJ has a passion for creative expression in many forms. She sings with Sound Circle, an internationally recognized women's a cappella ensemble, and has been a founding member since 1994. She also dances with the Body Mantra community in Boulder. These two communities are life-sustaining for her emotionally, spiritually, physically, and mentally.

She facilitates retreats and workshops that include the art of collage for individuals, families, and groups on various subjects, including the Art of Conscious Completion. BJ was a faculty member of the Boulder Center for Conscious Living where she taught classes on journaling, urban mysticism, completion, and collage as a deep means of self exploration and creative expression.

She continues to enjoy her private practice of over two decades in body-centered psychotherapy and is currently attending the Fourth North American, Three-Year Program in Shamanic Studies with Michael Harner's Foundation of Shamanic Studies, California. BJ can be found at her local haunt, writing and sipping a cappuccino, when she's not otherwise engaged.

BJ is living her good life with her Beloved partner and two children in Boulder, Colorado. To invite BJ to do a workshop in your area or for more information on her offerings, you may contact her at:

BJ Brown

 Wolfheals Shamanic Services
www.wolfheals.com
303.808.4006